HOW TO DISAPPEAR

ERASE YOUR DIGITAL FOOTPRINT, LEAVE FALSE TRAILS, AND VANISH WITHOUT A TRACE

Frank M. Ahearn and Eileen C. Horan

LYONS PRESS
Guilford, Connecticut
An imprint of Globe Pequot Press

Lyons Press is an imprint of Globe Pequot Press.

Text design: Bret Kerr | Smoke image © Veer Images
Layout artist: Melissa Evarts
Project editor: Kristen Mellitt

Library of Congress Cataloging-in-Publication Data is available on file.

ISBN 978-1-59921-977-6

Printed in the United States of America

10 9 8

TABLE OF CONTENTS

**All war is deception.
—Sun Tzu**

1

I'M FRANK. NICE TO MEET YOU.

YOU'RE READING THIS BOOK FOR ONE OF TWO REASONS: YOU WANT to vanish without a trace, or you're curious about what it would take.

I met a guy like you once.[1] He caught my eye in a bookstore in New Jersey where I like to people-watch from time to time. He was nervous, looking all around, picking up book after book about personal privacy and offshore banking. Then he wandered to the travel section and pulled out a guide to Costa Rica. He never even noticed me, the unassuming guy with a gray ponytail and sunglasses trailing him about a dozen yards behind.

We got in line to check out at the same time. He fidgeted in place, not realizing the same guy was still behind him. He finally got up to the cashier, and I watched with a raised eyebrow as he paid for his books with a credit card.

Big mistake, I thought. I wondered if he was really trying to disappear. I sincerely hoped he wasn't, because if that was the case, he had just left anyone trying to find him a big, fat clue.

After checking out, he made his way upstairs to the cafe. I followed him, grabbing a latte as I watched him settle into a corner table and obliviously thumb through his purchases.

What an idiot. Doesn't he know there are cameras everywhere? Doesn't he know how easy it is to trick a security guard into giving

---

1 Although I've changed some details about our meeting, of course.

you camera footage if you say the right things (and who cares if those things are true as long as they get results)? What if someone who was looking for him decided to do just that? I sort of felt bad for the poor bastard. If he had a good reason for wanting to disappear, or if he was in real trouble, he didn't stand a chance.

That's when a lightbulb went off in my head. I decided that I wasn't going to let this guy screw himself over. I could help him. After tossing my latte into the garbage, I walked right up to his table, said hello, shook his hand, and asked if I could sit down and talk to him for a minute.

Startled, he agreed.

I told him that my name was Frank M. Ahearn and that for many years I had worked as something called a "skip tracer." Clients paid me thousands of dollars to find people who were trying to hide: jailbirds, deadbeats, subpoenaed witnesses, the threatened and fearful, and just about anyone else you could think of who was trying to hide for whatever reasons they might have. Some of the people who hired me were tabloid editors trying to get their hands on celebrities. When they wanted to talk to some kids who had spent the night with Michael Jackson at Neverland, they called me. When they wanted to monitor O. J. Simpson's bank accounts, they called me. I once was hired to find Ozzy Osbourne's private telephone numbers for a paparazzo. I found all eight of them. I was hired to find George Harrison as he languished on his death bed. He was in New Jersey. My work fostered countless tabloid covers and brought a whole lot of criminals to justice.

I told the guy that the people I went after usually made my job easy. No matter how hard they tried to hide, they always slipped up, invariably doing something to give themselves away. Some big mistake would lead me to their location inside of an hour or two. Exceptions were rare.

I gestured at the pile of books the guy had spread out on the table and told him that if he was trying to hide, he had already made a fatal mistake. Since he'd bought all of these books with his credit card, they could easily be traced. Finding his location would be child's play for any skip tracer worth his salary.

 Here's my first piece of advice for all you would-be disappearing artists: Don't buy this book with a credit card. (But please do buy it!)

That white guy turned even whiter. He wasn't just idly curious about disappearing. He was serious. Or at least he thought he was.

So I kept talking. I explained how I or another skip tracer would track him down. I'd call up his credit card company under a false pretense, claiming to be him, saying that I needed to go over "my" recent credit card purchases and giving some made-up reason that sounded compelling. The customer service rep would then read me all the charges the guy had recently made, including the bookstore purchases. I'd say thank you, hang up, and call the bookstore and persuade whichever clerk picked up to tell me what "I" had bought with my credit card. I'd provide him with a transaction number or the name and address of a frequent-shopper account.

Once I knew the name of the books he'd purchased, I told the guy, I would have a pretty good idea of where he was headed. After that, I'd begin calling the airlines—US Airways, Copa, American, all the companies that served Costa Rica—until I'd located his flight information. Then I'd look at customer records for car rental companies around the airport in San José. If he'd put down his real name and address, I'd be able to find the location of his hotel in minutes. I'd call up the repo company or the Mafia or whoever had hired me, tell them where he was, and he could say *sayonara* to his great new life.

You could see the "oh fuck" in his eyes. He was dazed—I'd obviously just shot his grand disappearing plan to hell. But he was grateful. He asked for my phone number and said he wanted to call me to continue the conversation. We shook hands and went our separate ways.

I left the bookstore and drove to my office, where my business partner Eileen Horan was banging away on her computer, trying to find all the people we'd been hired to locate that day. I told her what had just happened with the guy in the bookstore. After laughing about his dumb mistake with the credit card, we started to talk about how he *really* should be handling that move to Costa Rica.

That got us thinking. Was this guy doomed no matter what he did? Was it possible to disappear without a trace? Could someone who's disappeared ever really feel confident that no one would find him, not even professionals like us?

We went over everything we would do to throw a smart pursuer off his trail. First, we'd delete or destroy all the information that was out there on him, or at least make it damn hard to find. Then we'd concoct a bunch of deceptive leads that would send the pursuer on a wild-goose chase. Finally, we'd build a new life for him quickly and quietly, using a series of anonymous private mailboxes and prepaid phones. Because Eileen and I used public records, credit reports, utility statements, and people-search Web sites to do most of our skip-tracing work, we'd be pretty much out of luck if those records were misleading or unavailable. We figured most other skip tracers would be, too.

As we talked, we realized we were onto something. We had valuable advice to give people who wanted to disappear. Plenty of books on the topic were available to the curious, but none of them talked about the flip side of the coin: the people like me and Eileen who would stop at nothing to find someone if the price was right. As long as our skip-tracing techniques and tricks remained a secret, no one had a prayer of outsmarting us.

That was good for our business, but bad for our targets' privacy and freedom. We thought law-abiding citizens deserved the chance to cut off contact with their past and begin a newer, more discreet life if that's what they chose to do. And we could help them do it. Why not start a disappearing business?

I'll be honest with you: This new business prospect excited us for all sorts of high-minded moral reasons, but we were also getting antsy about the kind of shit we had to pull to bring home the bacon. Every day, it seemed like another technique we used to find someone—such as calling up a cell phone company and pretending to be a customer or calling up a bank and lying our way into someone's account—was officially becoming illegal. Neither of us had ever been busted, but the cops had been giving us the side eye for a while, and we felt as if our time was running out. And ever since a little run-in we liked to call the helicopter incident, we had been especially paranoid.

A couple of years back, Eileen and I had been living together in a house by a canal in Florida. We were working at our computers when the sound no fed-fearing skip tracer wants to hear suddenly filled the office: CH-CH-CH-CH-CH. It was the sound of a helicopter overhead.

Eileen and I looked at each other. Then we stuck our heads out the window and looked up. Jesus. A helicopter was thirty fucking feet over our roof. We yanked our heads back in and began to run around like chickens with our heads cut off. I yelled at her to grab the phone book and find the name of a lawyer and said I would dial half the number, and when the police smashed down our door, we could dial the rest.

Eileen looked out our front door and saw police cars speeding by. We thought that maybe they had overlooked our driveway. We might still have a few minutes. So while she tore through the yellow pages looking for a lawyer, I threw a laptop to the ground and started stomping on it. Then I yanked open a drawer full of prepaid cell phones and calling cards, stuffed them all into a bucket, and ran out onto our lanai, flinging everything into the canal. My logic was this: If I was already going to jail, it wasn't as though I'd get that much extra time for destroying evidence. And did I have some evidence to destroy.

More minutes passed. Eileen and I pounded away on all of our equipment until everything was either in little pieces or underwater. The helicopter was still there. Why hadn't they come to the door? "Fuck this," said Eileen. "I'm going to go for a bike ride to figure everything out." She snuck out the back way.

Fifteen minutes later, she was back. I will never forget the look on her face.

"You are not going to believe this," she said.

"What?" I said.

"There's a fucking manatee lost in the canals. It wasn't the police, it was the park police."

I looked down at the equipment smashed all over my floor, probably $5,000 worth of stuff, plus all the time we spent cramming our hard drives full of files. And would you believe it wasn't even the first time I'd destroyed everything I owned on a false alarm?

Yep, it's time to get out of this business, I thought.

I HOPE YOU CAN SEE WHY EILEEN AND I WERE EXCITED AT THE prospect of a new, slightly less risky line of work. If we were helping people disappear, we would no longer have to go bat shit every time some manatee stranded itself in the canal. So back to that day in New Jersey. Eileen and I sincerely hoped the man from the bookstore would call. And we were more than delighted when he did.

When Ed Nothisrealname called, he asked if he could hire us to help him sneak out of the country undetected. As I had suspected, he wasn't just curious about disappearing—he really did want to skip town, and he had a good reason for it, too. Turns out he was a whistleblower who had received money from the government for revealing illegal practices in his company. He was in no trouble with the feds but was concerned that his former bosses were out for revenge. Ed had planned on heading to Costa Rica, but his run-in with me in the bookstore had given him second thoughts.

Eileen and I took the job. We wrote down all the disappearing techniques we had talked about earlier and walked our brand-new client through our system one step at a time, showing him what to do. First, we altered or changed all the records that existed about him, including, of course, the frequent-buyer account he had at the bookstore where I met him. We created a bunch of false trails for his pursuers to follow, opening up accounts and persuading real estate companies to run checks on his credit in foreign countries where he had no interest in living.

Finally, we sent him to his new home in the most complicated way possible, putting him on a plane to Canada to fly to Jamaica to hop a puddle jumper to Anguilla, where he opened a bank account that he only kept temporarily. We opened an international corporation for him so he could bank anonymously and transferred his money over and over through a tangle of bank accounts until it wasn't clear where it had come from. Eventually, he and his money landed in Belize, safe and sound.

Our strategy worked. As I write this, Ed is still in the Caribbean living off his windfall. His bosses haven't found him. And he has a killer tan. All thanks to a chance encounter in a New Jersey bookstore.

ED WAS JUST THE BEGINNING. I NOW HAD A NEW CALLING IN LIFE. Instead of pursuing people for hire, I began to devote my life to the pursued. I worked with middle-aged guys who dreamed of getting away from their bad marriages, back taxes, and mooching grown-up kids. I worked with frightened stalking victims desperate to stay safe. I worked with men and women whose personal information had been compromised, and showed them how to take that information away from prying eyes.

Here's who I didn't help: cops, criminals, or crazies. I laughed away the young hotshots who wanted to hide their assets from the IRS, ignored rambling e-mails from schizophrenics convinced they were being bugged by the FBI, and said no thanks to a whole lot of undercover cops and kooks who believed I ran some kind of international crime syndicate.

If you're one of these people, by the way—a cop, a criminal, or a crazy—this book is not going to help you, so you should probably just put it back on the shelf. Oh, what the hell, go ahead and buy it. Just don't try to contact me.

Business was good but didn't go gangbusters until the day I wrote an article about disappearing for EscapeArtist.com, a Web site on offshore living. From that day on, Eileen's and my inboxes were overflowing with e-mail. People wrote from Finland, Bali, Canada, Russia, China, Tokyo, Australia, Europe, and South America. It seemed everyone in the world wanted to know how to disappear. We'd struck some international nerve.

Foreign governments took interest, too. I was surprised to discover that the Canadian government froze all of the assets I held in its country after reading my article. Apparently it freaked them out. If you're reading this, Canada: I am not a crook. And unlike Nixon, I mean it.

As of this writing, I've helped more than a hundred people disappear. The demand for my advice has grown even more since the economic meltdown, as CEOs jump sinking ships and laid-off workers spring for the beach life they've always dreamed about. Demand is so high that I'm able to charge serious money for what I do. In this book, I'm going to give it to you for much less. Consider it my payback to society, or karma, for all the crazy stuff I did back in the day.

I sure did a lot of crazy stuff. Back when I was a skip tracer, I was one of the best people hunters to walk the streets. And as I said, I wasn't always what you would call aboveboard. I caught tens of thousands of people by calling their banks, their phone companies, their mothers, their sisters, their friends. I'd chat up a few customer service representatives or coax a few nuggets of information out of family members and could get a target location so fast your head would spin. And, as I said to my very first disappearing client, most of my skip-tracing targets were disturbingly easy to find. Instead of taking the time to disappear properly, they just got up and went, and they used their credit cards or their frequent-flier accounts on their way out the door. Morons.

This book is my master class on how to disappear while avoiding the same mistakes they made. I'm not judging your reasons for wanting to disappear. You might have a perfectly legitimate reason for wanting privacy. Maybe you just won the lottery and want to protect your windfall. Maybe you're a witness who's not getting much support from the feds. Maybe you're an abused spouse or just an ordinary citizen who wants to know what's out there on you and how to protect that information from would-be thieves. You could also be an aspiring international jewel thief who's always on the lookout for new ideas. (Don't worry. No judgment.)

You're up against a formidable foe. Whoever is after you—be it an old employer, creditor, or identity thief—might hire a private investigator or skip tracer like me to find you, and if that happens, you're in big trouble. Skip tracers are career liars who will pretend to be you or a close friend or family member so they can eke out everything customer service representatives, clerks, receptionists, and even your loved ones know about you. The only way to defend yourself against this deception is to counter with a little of your own. That's the key behind all of my advice for disappearing successfully: Fight deception with deception.

But before you know how to fight, you have to know what you're fighting. So let me tell you a little bit more about how the world of skip tracing works.

2

MEET YOUR ENEMY: THE SKIP TRACER

FOR MUCH OF MY CAREER, I FOUND PEOPLE BY LYING TO EXTRACT information from phone companies and banks and even law enforcement. Most of the techniques I used in the past are extremely illegal now, so I'm not recommending you try them. But it's worth knowing about them anyway, because if someone is seriously after you, he's probably not going to care whether he's breaking the law. In this chapter, I'm going to teach you six big principles of skip tracing by telling you some stories from my own life.

> **Skip tracer, n.:** a person who tracks people down and uncovers private information for a living. Targets include jailbirds, deadbeats, subpoenaed witnesses, and just about anyone else who's trying to hide.

You can sum up my whole career in three words: liar for hire. People ask me how I got into this business, and my standard reply is, "I was unemployable pretty much everywhere else." It's the truth. When I found skip tracing, I felt as though I'd found my calling. Successful skip tracers like Eileen and me can make the person on the other end of the phone believe anything and thereby extract all the information we need.

I was good at manipulating the hell out of my targets back when I first got into the business, in my twenties. In those days, I worked undercover at retail stores, trying to bust employees for stealing. I eventually got bored with low-stakes store work, so I made a deal with the boss at my investigative agency: If I could get my hands on his private phone records, he would move me up from those undercover ops to a desk in the back office doing real skip tracing. He smiled and told me that if I found his phone records, not only would he give me the job, but he'd fire the skip tracer he had.

That night, I hit a pay phone and started contacting phone companies, searching for my boss's long distance carrier. When I hit the right one, I claimed to be my boss. I said I needed to go over my phone usage for the past month. The only thing the phone company rep wanted me to do was verify the address on file, which I knew. After a pause, the rep started reading off area codes and phone numbers. My pretext had worked perfectly.

> **Pretext, n.:** a lie or misleading excuse given to trick someone into providing sensitive information. In the above story, I offered the pretext that I was my boss and needed to know my phone records.

> **To pretext, v.:** the act of finding out information through deception.

The next day, I walked into the office and up to my boss and dropped the yellow pad of scribbled numbers onto his desk. He picked up the sheets, glanced at my notes, and immediately knew what he was holding. That very Friday the guy in the back room was fired, and boom! There was a new skip tracer in town.

That boss and I eventually had creative differences, shall we say, so I left that company and started my own. I quickly felt at home in the investigative underworld, where there was (and still is) a thriving illegal marketplace for personal information. People buy it, sell it, and trade it.

Which brings me to the first principle of skip tracing:

 Your personal information is a valuable commodity, no matter who you are, and there will always be people interested in having it.

This applies to law-abiding citizens as well as criminals. Whether someone wants to find you or just steal your identity, that person is willing to pay big bucks for the ability to do it.

Once I discovered how much money people's personal information was worth, I got into the information-brokering business. I initially started out as a broker, buying information from some people and selling it to others, but after some of my sources became unreliable, I decided to go straight to the source and pretext my own info. I was great at getting the valuable stuff: criminal records, Social Security numbers, that kind of thing. And I'd do it no questions asked, if the price was right.

A TYPICAL CELEBRITY SKIP TRACE

A few years ago, George Clooney said something nasty about the tabloids in an interview, calling them the scum of the earth or something. Nowadays he says stuff like that about the paparazzi a lot, as you know if you read any of those magazines regularly. (I know, you only read the tabloids when you're in line at the grocery store, right?)

Well, wouldn't you know I got a fax in my fax machine later that day with simple instructions: FIND GEORGE CLOONEY. Note to celebrities: Insult the tabloids, and they'll only hound you harder. (Maybe that's why George Clooney keeps insulting them!)

At the height of my skip-tracing career, I was earning money by the truckload—sometimes up to $10,000 a week. I had the money to rent an office and hire ten people to support me, including Eileen, the bookkeeper who eventually became my business partner and coauthor. We extracted information for tabloids, and two or three times a week, we'd get an assignment to dig up dirt on some of the biggest names in the country.

My days started with coffee and a pile of faxes requesting phone records on one subject, a bank record for another, maybe a criminal record for a third. If your name came across my desk, you were in for one bad ride. I'd sit down and think about what I knew about you and where you had probably left clues about your whereabouts: utility companies, grocery stores, frequent-flier clubs. Then I'd pick up the phone and start pretexting.

I was the best in the business. I succeeded because I had a devious and creative mind and I could think outside the box about how to persuade people to give me what I wanted.

That's leads me to a second principle of skip tracing:

 The information trade is just like any other business. The people who succeed have the cleverness to spot gaps in the market and the balls to fill those gaps themselves. The constant competition among skip tracers causes the good ones to get better and better every year.

Plenty of people are willing to take their skills to the next level to get your private information for someone who's paying them good money to do it, and fighting those people takes constant vigilance.

Sometimes I felt like MacGyver when I went out on assignment—like the time a client offered me $2,000 if I could find out whether ten random people had criminal records. I figured out how to do it in fifteen minutes using a child's beach sand pail, some pay phones, and a whole bunch of quarters. Here's what I did: I carried the red plastic bucket to a peep show in Times Square, which was more seedy than touristy in those days, and exchanged a twenty and a ten for $30 in quarters from the change machine. Then I left, making my way eight blocks south to Penn Station. I parked myself in one of its many rows of pay phone banks, which are now all gone. Getting comfortable, I dialed a police station in the South Bronx and got some cop on the line.

I identified myself as Detective Christopher from Midtown South and explained that our teletype was down and I needed him to run some names for me. He sounded unhappy with the request and asked for a call-back number. I gave him one. It just so happened to be the number of the pay phone in the empty booth beside me.

A few seconds later, that phone rang, and changing my voice, I answered, "Midtown South." The cop asked for Detective Christopher. I told him to hold, covering the mouthpiece of the phone so he couldn't hear the train departures blaring over the loudspeaker. I caught a few stares from people passing by.

"His line is busy," I said. "Wanna leave a message?" He said "no" and hung up. Then he came back on the first phone and said, "Whatcha need, Christopher?"

Two thousand dollars were mine. Boy, had this high school dropout found the right line of work.

I HOPE THAT STORY SHOWS YOU THAT SKIP TRACERS CAN BE PRETTY creative. It also illustrates a third key point about skip tracing:

 If there's accurate information on you out there for skip tracers to find, they will find it, provided they have enough time and money.

Think about it—I was talking to a cop, and the whole scam took me fifteen minutes. Even if that particular cop hadn't given me the goods, all I would have had to do was keep chipping away at police stations around the city. Every "no" eventually leads to a "yes," and

---

FRANK'S RULES FOR SKIP TRACING

- I could extract anything I wanted from a customer service representative on the phone, with the right attitude . . . or for the right price. Every no eventually led to a yes.

- When I picked up the phone, I really believed I was who I claimed to be. As George Costanza said, "It's not a lie if you believe it!" I wasn't afraid to get arrogant and ask for a supervisor if someone questioned my story.

- I schmoozed *a lot*. If I was on the phone with an older woman, I told her my daughter was getting married. If it was a young guy, I shot the shit about my recent trip to the Caribbean with the boys or sucking down beer at a wet T-shirt contest. I took customer service reps away from their day to create a quick bond.

- When I called a company and received an automated system, I pressed 0, the magic button for a real person. When I got someone on the line, I did the Skip Trace Stutter. I said I c-c-couldn't use the automated system because of my condition, and then I pretexted away. Or I busted out some Tourette's syndrome. There was nothing like five "fucks" in a row to make someone want to get me off the phone as soon as possible. Boy, I'm going to hell, aren't I?

- I never asked straight out for what I needed. I didn't say, "Hey, can I get my account number?" or "What's my address again?" Instead, I devised elaborate setups so that my mark gave me the information I needed almost as an afterthought.

---

if my employer had had enough money to hire me for several days, I could have found much more than just those folks' criminal records. I could have had their credit and bank records, for instance. And more.

In fact, skip tracing has only become easier and more efficient over the years. There aren't many pay phones around anymore, but you can pretext anywhere, anytime with two of those prepaid cell phones you can buy at any wireless store. No trip to the peep show needed. You don't even have to be good with computers, although it doesn't hurt. People ask me all the time how many computer languages I know. The answer is zero. I know one language: pretext!

Finding out information is easy if you have the guts. That's the reality behind the fourth principle:

 As long as companies have real live customer service representatives—and as a consumer, I hope they always do—all a good skip tracer needs is charm and a telephone.

The best skip tracers can get whatever they want once they get a real person on the line. You'd be amazed at the organizations I've successfully pretexted with simple conversations: Scotland Yard, Interpol, and police stations and banks all over America. These days, I've retired from the world of skip tracing, but plenty of people like me are still out there, talking to service reps and schmoozing for the goods.

Let's look at the kind of social engineering a skip tracer might do tomorrow if you've fled for a palm-tree lifestyle and he or she's been hired to find you. First, the skip tracer will plunk down $20 for a prepaid cell phone and $19.95 for one of those online information searches that anyone can find by entering "background check" on Google. Those Web sites never ask why you're looking for information about someone.

MY CONVERSATION WITH SCOTLAND YARD

GUY AT SCOTLAND YARD: *Hello?*

ME: *Hi, this is Pat Brown calling from the NYC joint task force. I have a bit of a problem here. I'm working on this launched [i.e., stolen] jewelry case, and I have an individual's name but it might be an alias. I'm hoping you have this information.*

GUY AT SCOTLAND YARD: *Why don't you talk to [French name], this associate of mine at Interpol? He'll help you out.*

Yep. Cracking international law enforcement is just that easy. The same joint-task-force pretext worked with customs offices, too. They just assumed I was a police officer.

That site might give the skip tracer an old address, the names of your relatives, or old phone numbers. If she finds an old address, she might start calling nearby bookstores using a prepaid phone. After a few calls, she'll stumble on the store where you bought all those books to plan your great escape, and she'll say:

SKIP TRACER: *Hi, this is Pat Cooper over at the credit department. Our systems are down, and I had a few names disappear out of the system. Can you check to see if a customer named Jimmy Chris has a discount card with us?*

[The bookstore clerk would typically ask the skip tracer to hold on, and the clerk would check.]

CLERK: *Yes, we have a customer by the name of Jimmy Chris.*

SKIP TRACER: *Great. Is he on 13 Ritz Lane?*

CLERK: *That would be him.*

SKIP TRACER: *What I need you to do is take a few minutes and go over his purchases. I think some of Mr. Chris's purchases got deleted from his account.*

CLERK: *We show he purchased a travel book to Costa Rica, a book about offshore banking, and Dr. Seuss's* Oh, the Places You'll Go!

SKIP TRACER: *Thanks for your help. Have a great day.*

CLERK: *You too!*

SKIP TRACER: *Oh, one other thing. Did he list an e-mail address? I just want to let him know that we've fixed his account and send him a coupon.*

CLERK: *Yes: _____@yahoo.com.*

The skip tracer will now know that you've purchased travel and offshore books. That would be a great lead to a skip tracer. She'll have your e-mail address as well. Maybe she'll hit Netflix next and discover that you have *The Seasoned Traveler: Panama* in your queue. If you're actually in Panama, you're done.

It all sounds too simple to be real, doesn't it? But I promise you—this is really how skip tracing works. Not many people have the guts to call up random companies pretending to be someone else, so the people on the other end of the line rarely think to ask questions when that happens. Even scarier is the fact that these tactics work with everyone—not just morons in customer service, but your friends and family members, too. That's a fifth principle of skip tracing:

 A good skip tracer will be able to get information from anyone who has it.

That includes your neighbor, your housekeeper, and even your mother. If you don't believe me, here are a couple of stories to set you straight.

One time, a frequent client called me up and gave me the name of a woman. All he wanted to know was her location. Simple enough. Eileen and our assistant Karen and I banged away at the usual places for information, pretexting phone companies and other sources pretending to be this woman. Before long, we figured out where the woman was likely holed up.

Next, I made a phone call to the woman's possible location. Her housekeeper answered the phone, and the conversation went something like this.

HOUSEKEEPER: *Hello?*

ME: *Hi, this is Pat Brown with UPS. We have a water-damaged package for [the woman, whose name I intentionally mispronounced.]*

HOUSEKEEPER: *Umm.*

ME: *It's going to need a signature, so I was wondering when she'd be back.*

HOUSEKEEPER: *Uhh.*

ME: *That's OK. I'll just send the package back.*

HOUSEKEEPER: *[Pause]*

ME: *Should I go ahead and do that?*

HOUSEKEEPER: *No . . . no. You can deliver it here.*

ME: *OK, when should we come by for a signature?*

HOUSEKEEPER: *She'll be back around six.*

Thank you and click. I called my client and relayed the information that the subject would be at such-and-such location at a certain time. "So who's the woman?" I asked.

"Watch the news," he told me.

Later, as I sipped a beer at my local bar, a newsflash about Bill Clinton and a possible affair with a White House intern lit the screen. My eyes popped. Oh, shit. Seems we had hunted down Monica Lewinsky.

THEN THERE WAS THE TIME WHEN A CLIENT BY THE NAME OF MR. Benny—who was in the waste removal business, if you know what I mean—asked me to find out "everything" about some person. "What do you mean everything?" I asked.

"Fuckin' everyding," he said. "Whud, you don't hear?"

I said I heard him, but I didn't know what he meant by "everything."

"Don't be an asshole," he said. "Nobuddy likes an asshole. Everything is everything." He hung up.

Nothing was worse than a client who said he needed everything— well, maybe it was worse when the client was on a limited budget. Mr. Benny never had a budget. I never sent him an invoice, either. I was paid in cash at the same time and place on the first of every month in Manhattan, and if I missed the drop, too bad for me.

I ran a Skip Tracer's Trifecta of searches: a motor vehicle search, a credit report, and a criminal background check. (Most investigators start with those three searches.) Then I tried the utility companies. I searched and searched and searched. This guy was a nothing. He lived in the ass end of New Jersey and was an unemployed union worker with a drinking problem.

Literally all I had was his date of birth, his past-due utility bills, and his mother's address and phone number. I was racking my brain until I realized that his birthday was a month away. I jumped up, grabbed my trusty bucket of quarters, and hit a coin phone on Route 17 in Jersey. Pouring the quarters in the box, I heard the sound of ringing and then a very sweet hello from his mother.

"Hi, Mrs. Jones," I said. "This is Pat Brown. I don't know if you remember me, but I work with your son in Newark." Without hesitation, she said she remembered me and that it'd been too long since we last met and oh how the time flies. I'm sure bullshitting an old lady is a sin somewhere, but a man's gotta make a living.

"Next month we are going to throw your son a birthday party," I said. "We are throwing him a *This Is Your Life* surprise party."

"Oh, how *nice!*" she said. She thought me and my buddies were the best in the world, since her son was down on his luck. She gave me one of those side-of-the-mouth whispers: "You know, it's the ponies. That's where his money goes."

I wondered if he owed Mr. Benny big money but realized that if that were true, one of his legs would already be snapped in half. So I said, "What I need from you, if you don't mind, is if you could take some time and tell me about his life."

Mrs. Jones started with kindergarten and moved to summer camp, his first girlfriend, his first job, high school, vacations to the Poconos, his best friends, his favorite sports team, his hospital stays, and on and on and on. Finally, I was down to my last ten quarters and took the pretext to the present: the what and when and where of his life now. There was still nothing of interest except a hot model girlfriend.

I drove to a peep show twenty-five minutes away and got a new batch of quarters to call Mr. Benny. Turns out the girlfriend was the problem. She'd just dumped Mr. Benny, and he was pissed off. He was also pissed at *me*, because I'd failed to find out something pretty big about Mr. Lost-It-All-on-the-Ponies: His dad and Mr. Benny had been in the slammer together. Oops. For some reason, his mom failed to mention that.

WE SKIP TRACERS DO MAKE MISTAKES SOMETIMES. WE'LL FAIL TO GET some crucial piece of information, as I did with Mr. Benny's mark, or we'll say something on the phone that raises the suspicions of the person we're talking to. Sometimes we'll get the wrong information from a bogus source. But we don't have to worry that our mistakes will come back to haunt us, since we use prepaid phones and credit cards and protect ourselves with other tactics, such as only using public wireless Internet. And there you have the final principle of skip tracing:

Skip tracers can make as many mistakes as they want when they're trying to find you. All you need to make is one.

In fact, our mistakes can be a lot of fun. They make great stories. One time, for instance, a tabloid reporter called me up to find out John Ritter's private phone number. (This was back when he was still alive, of course.) I called up all the utility companies in his area and began each call: "Hi, I'm John Ritter . . ." Finally I hit pay dirt: a company Ritter had an account with.

The guy on the other end of the phone was thrilled. He said something like this: "John Ritter?! *The* John Ritter? I love your work!"

"Hey, thanks!" I said. Then, in case he could see my out-of-state phone number, I added, "I'm out on location for a movie and confused about my bill for this month's utilities. I wanted to see whether you had my contact information or my agent's because I don't know where my bills are going."

"I think we have your home address," the guy on the phone said. He was all flustered.

"Great, so you have . . ." I started saying John's home address.

"Yep."

"And what are the phone numbers on file?"

"Let's see, they're . . ." He read out a home number and then a cell. Bingo.

Then came the verbal diarrhea. The guy kept talking and talking: about "my" career, *Three's Company*, that kind of thing. He was a *huge* John Ritter fan. I decided to keep shooting the shit with him. Why not?

We talked and talked about movies and TV, and finally he wrapped up: "Hey, listen, I just loved your dad's work, too."

"Thanks!" I said. "I'll tell him you said that."

There was a deadly pause on the other end of the line.

"I thought your dad was dead," the guy said.

Click went the phone.

I couldn't stop laughing. It was no problem for me. All I had to do was give John's number to my client, throw out my prepaid cell phone, and never think about it again.

As I hope you can see, skip tracing can be an entertaining career. I'm not encouraging you to go into the business—as I said, most of this stuff is very illegal now, and pretexting a bank will land you in the slammer for a long time if you're caught. But lots of people still do this stuff, so remember the six principles I just taught you:

- Your personal information is a valuable commodity, no matter who you are. At some point, someone will come looking for it.
- Skip tracing is a business just like any other, and the constant competition among the people who work in the field causes them to outdo themselves and become better and better every year.
- If there is *any* accurate information out there for skip tracers to find, they will probably find it . . . if they've been paid enough.
- All skip tracers need to succeed are charm and a telephone.
- A good skip tracer will be able to get information out of anyone who has it, no matter how much those people love you and have your best interest at heart.
- Skip tracers can make dozens of mistakes. You don't have the luxury of making even one.

So if you want to disappear from your life—or you're fine where you are, but you want to take your information away from the eyes of would-be thieves and stalkers—you need to prepare an exit strategy that takes these six principles as a given.

Read on and I'll help you with that strategy. But before I do, I want to call attention to your biggest liabilities. There are certain places where you should begin your disappearing act *today*.

3

A SKIP TRACER'S BEST FRIENDS

IF YOU'RE LUCKY, YOU'RE ABLE TO AFFORD WATER AND POWER AND all the other utilities that make life comfortable. If you're luckier, you can afford a computer, too. It opens up a whole new world of fun: chats with friends on Facebook and Twitter, fast and easy online banking, great online customer service from your phone company and your electric company and all those other big companies. (Isn't it great what the recession has done for customer service? Companies are falling all over themselves to be as user-friendly as possible, with improved Web sites, 24-7 help lines, personal attention. . . . Yep, it's a great time to be alive.)

Especially if you're a skip tracer.

This chapter is all about why customer-friendly companies are not your friends. Also, you need to know that social media sites are the worst thing to happen to privacy since J. Edgar Hoover. Here's the number one thing you should know if you're trying to live discreetly:

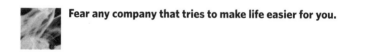

Fear any company that tries to make life easier for you.

These days, that's pretty much every company. But I'm thinking especially about the Web sites that make finding all your old high school friends a cinch if you upload all your e-mail contacts and write down your address and phone number and post personal pictures of your self and your family on-line for the world to see. I'm also thinking about online phone books, blogs, interactive sites, and viral-marketing ad campaigns. I'm particularly thinking about the big national utility, phone, and Internet companies that outsource you to some call center in India or rural Kentucky when you call them with a question. Those call center guys are a breeze to pretext.

The easier it is for a customer to get a real voice on the line, the easier it is for that customer's stalker to do real damage. If a company assures you that you're not just an anonymous user to it . . . tread carefully.

If you want to stay private, your first step is to take down your Facebook. Stop posting on Classmates. Delete your Tweets. I can't believe I even have to say this—staying off social media should be a no-brainer if you want to disappear—but I've caught so many people using my skip-tracing skills on social media sites that it bears repeating:

 Social networks and viral media are privacy's worst enemies.

As I said in the last chapter, skip tracing is an old-fashioned people business. You don't need to be a hacker to find someone's personal information online. You don't need passwords, either. Those never hurt, but we skip tracers can get by just fine without them. Our careers are centered on what we call "**social engineering.**"

Social engineering, n.: 1. the act of acquiring sensitive information through cunning and conversation rather than brute force, trespass, or digital intrusion. 2. the study of cajoling information out of people.

Social engineer, n.: one who practices social engineering.

The first thing a skip tracer will do when he's on your tail is try to tap into your network of friends. He'll find the names of businesses you frequent, places you hang out, and people you spend time with. Then he'll start making calls and sending e-mails until he can trick someone into giving him information. Social networking makes this whole process a one-stop shop.

If you are on Facebook, your page will be a gold mine, even if it's set to private. Keep in mind that unless you've changed your privacy preferences to the strictest settings, strangers will be able to see your friends list, even if they haven't "friended" you. Oh, but you can only see a handful of friends, you say. Right, but if you keep hitting "Reload," that handful will change every time. My colleagues and I have found so many of our targets' family members and coworkers that way that we have a special name for it: the Facebook Refresh.

Facebook is a real treasure trove for us. But it's not the only site we use.

A-Z OF STUPID PLACES TO SPEND YOUR TIME

AIM	Mixx	Tumblr
Bebo	MySpace	Twitter
Blogger	Netvibes	TypePad
Classmates	Orkut	Vimeo
Delicious	Picasa	WordPress
Digg	Propeller	Xanga
Flickr	Reddit	YouTube
Google Talk	RSS	Ziki
LinkedIn	StumbleUpon	

All social networking sites offer juicy information. No matter what you've chosen to put on the Internet, a good skip tracer will be able to use it against you. He'll probably "friend" your friends and family, pretending to be an acquaintance looking to get in touch. With this in mind, remember:

 You never know if the people on your "friends" list are real.

If you say yes to people on a social site, even if they're old friends, be sure to call them up or write them a note thanking them for the add—as a way of confirming that they're the ones who really added you. This is especially true if it's someone you haven't talked to in years.

If you think you could never get scammed, listen to this story. Early on in the whole social media craze, Eileen and I were hired to bust a truck driver collecting disability for a bogus back injury. We'll call him Gary. The client who hired me had conducted surveillance on Gary but could never catch him in the act of fraud.

When Eileen and I set to work, everything came up blank at first. Gary appeared to be unemployed. Then Eileen Googled several variations of Gary's name, throwing in parts of his date of birth, and lo and behold: She discovered that Gary had posted a message on Classmates.com, searching for his long-lost high school girlfriend. Eileen posed as the girlfriend and contacted Gary with a backstory of a miserable marriage and how happy she was that Gary remembered her. Gary's response was fast and fulsome: He spilled out his love over what would have been several pages printed out.

After a few e-mails back and forth, the tone of Gary's messages became suspicious, and he said he wanted to talk on the phone. Eileen went deeper into the backstory, explaining that she had to be cautious of her abusive husband. Gary backed off, so we had more time.

Eileen began to feel guilty. Gary was living in a run-down trailer park outside of Vegas with a potbellied pig named Boris (I'm not making this up). He didn't even have his own computer; he used a computer at the library. In one e-mail, he wrote that he had once waited four hours in the library for her to e-mail him back.

I reminded Eileen that Gary was committing fraud and that we were going to make big money if we located where he worked. "Oh yeah," she said, then e-mailed Gary that she was working as a waitress and lived not too far from him. Although Gary started to open up about his life, he still would not mention anything about where he worked, and he actually stuck to his story about being on disability.

DO I FEEL GUILTY ABOUT ALL THIS?

I once gave a talk at Princeton University about my life as a skip tracer and my career helping people disappear. I remember one wide-eyed WASPy type raised his hand at the end of my talk and said, "Have you ever been in jail?" For a minute, I just stared at him, making him squirm. Then I answered. "No. No, I haven't."

Christ, was I ever a fish out of water at that place.

Another person asked me if I ever felt bad for hounding people and giving them up to insurance and credit companies and paparazzi and other not-so-nice clients. My response: I never went after innocent victims. If you were on my list, you'd done something stupid or illegal to get there. I did what I did to make money, but even I had my limits. All of my targets deserved to have their privacy raided—or they chose to forego their privacy by entering showbiz!

The e-mails dragged on, and one day Gary began asking about people from their past: Did she remember this one and that one? Seems Gary was still suspicious.

So we turned the tables on Gary. Eileen wrote that she was insulted and hurt by his mistrust and wanted to end the e-mail exchange. This shook Gary, who asked to meet. "Where?" Eileen asked. "I drive a Sin City bus to the casinos on the weekends—here is my route and schedule," he replied.

Our client, armed with a hidden camera, got a ride on Gary's bus. Gary had to serve time for disability fraud. Thank you, social networking.

A LOT OF PEOPLE LIKE GARY GO ON SOCIAL SITES TO PURSUE A specific interest—in his case, romance. Others go on to talk about Beanie Babies and knitting and ballroom dance and all that other crazy cat lady stuff. If you have a hobby like this, you should be getting out in the real world and joining a book club or a knitting circle, not joining a Listserv. Which brings me to my next point . . .

 Practice your hobbies in the real world, not online.

Just ask the lady we nabbed because of her obsession with Madonna. She had taken a fall and was collecting disability and suing her employer for negligence. The client believed that the injury was fake. Several private investigators attempted surveillances, but she was cautious and never did yard work or worked another job or did anything that would disprove her injury.

We ran her name on Google and found guest-book entries on Madonna fan sites. From there, we located her MySpace page, which was an homage to Madonna. We wrote to her that she had won a prize to compete with other winners for a spot in a Madonna video. We sent her a Web site and a phone number, both of which had a message about the contest. The Web site was registered offshore with a private registration paid via a prepaid credit card, and the phone number was for a prepaid cell phone, so there was no way she could have traced them back to our little operation—not even if she'd thought about doing it and knew how.

Soon the subject contacted us, and we replied with the rules and conditions of the Madonna video contest, which included a tryout. On audition day, she arrived and filled out paperwork claiming she was fit and able to participate. During the audition, we had her lift small weights and do a few jumping jacks, sit-ups, and dance moves—all on camera. On cue, she smiled for the camera and stated her name. Her case and claim were immediately dropped.

Every single time we skip tracers find out anything about a target's interests, we grin like idiots. They're the surest route to finding out the target's location. A bookworm will transfer his Amazon Prime account to his new address in Costa Rica. A filet fanatic will make sure Omaha Steaks has a current phone number. As soon as we know you have an interest, we can start making calls to the people who help you sustain it.

If you don't want someone to know every detail about your life, make sure you don't put your whole life on the Internet. Once again, I can't believe I have to say this, but:

 Think before you hit "publish." Even if you cancel your account later, what's done on the Internet can never be undone.

A client once gave us the résumé of a woman applying for a job at his company. We located her old LinkedIn profile. It listed a job that wasn't on the résumé she submitted, along with some troublingly conflicting dates. She did not get a job offer. Take the time to look back on the sites you've belonged to, even if you think you've deleted your presence there.

 Sometimes people have more than one LinkedIn profile and forget. Make sure you haven't made duplicates.

It's scary how much damage a Web page can do and how long those pages seem to stick around. But even scarier is the fundamental lack of control an individual has over his or her own page on a social networking site. Even if you're not in the network, your friends might be—and they might have published dirt on you without intending to.

The Internet is one of those damned-if-you-do, damned-if-you-don't places. Even if you've done nothing wrong, your friends and neighbors can put your private information out there and leave you vulnerable to people like me. They don't realize that they're doing any damage, you don't realize what's out there, and before you know it, the skip tracer or stalker or identity thief is at your door.

Family and friends, corporations and nonprofits just throw your personal information up on the Web without a second thought to protecting your privacy. If you don't believe me, just go to a Web site like Switchboard.com or Yahoo! People Search or BirthDatabase.com and see how much of your personal information is available there free of charge. Your address, your phone number, and probably your age are all there, if you haven't specifically asked those companies to take down your information.

Facebook and Twitter and Yahoo! are all well-meaning businesses. So are the utility and phone companies that bend over backward trying to beat the competition in customer service . . . and end up putting personal information within reach of anyone who thinks to extend an arm. Remember: Skip tracers are expert schmoozers who get most of your personal information by making old-fashioned phone calls. That means one thing:

 The kinder and nicer a company's customer service representative is, the easier it is to pretext.

These days, you can call up most of the big national utility and phone companies and get an address or account name in seconds. Say I had a phone number and wanted to find out who was using it. I could call up a utility company's customer service line, enter in the phone number, and a robotic voice would "confirm" the account by reciting your street number or last name. So much for protecting your privacy. Thank you, utility company.

WORST OFFENDERS

You're probably wondering which utility companies are particularly bad about keeping your information safe from skip tracers, stalkers, Al Qaeda, or the Mafia. I would never name names . . . oh wait, yes I would. Pacific Gas and Electric. Florida Power and Light Company.

If the robot didn't give me what I needed, maybe I'd just press 0—the skip tracer's magic button—and talk to a friendly customer service representative. Most of them are eager to help without much prompting. "I have not received my bill and need to know if I owe you anything," I'd say. The rep would do her thing and tell me I owed fifty bucks.

I'd ask for the mailing address she had on file: "Are you showing the bill going to my home address or P.O. box?" The rep would answer, "We show the home address."

I'd cut in before she had a moment to think. "Do they have the address down correctly? I didn't get the bill." She'd almost always follow with the wonderful words of "We've got 1005 Fairview Lane . . ." or something like that.

This worked most of the time. If it didn't, I'd take it a step further and say, "Do you have my correct home or work number?" Naturally, they would not know if the number on file was my home or work, and they'd read it off.

NOT ALL REPS ARE CREATED EQUAL

I'll probably get in trouble for saying this, but for some reason, male customer service reps give out information much more easily than women. Older women are the hardest to crack. Young women are a little easier.

Sometimes I can only establish a connection with older female reps by saying that they sound like my dear mother, who's just passed. Nothing like death to make someone uneasy and put them in a compassionate and helpful mode.

You know, my difficulty with older female reps could just be due to the fact that I'm a guy. The more naturally you can schmooze with someone, the easier he or she is to dupe. It's all about finding a connection with the person.

Pretty much any major national company with a customer service line will give out at least some of your private information if a skip tracer asks for it in the right way. Cable TV companies are easy to infiltrate: Like the utilities, they have prompt systems that will bring up accounts from any number of different data points they enter. It's been my experience that most cable companies keep account information by phone number, and most phone numbers are valid and up-to-date: If you want to watch a pay-per-view event, after all, your phone number has to be current.

When I skip-traced full time, I considered cable companies a backup in the event the phone and utility companies wouldn't put out. My coworkers and I would locate the local cable provider in the area and process the number through the prompt. If we got a hit, we would press zero to get a rep. "Hi, this is Pat Brown from cable repair dispatch. We are down and need you to bring up a number for service," I'd say. They'd bring up the number and give me the information.

Skip-tracing subjects via their cable accounts remains a recession favorite among my colleagues, since cable seems to be the one service people keep activated in the tough times. As with utility companies, each state has two or three large cable carriers, and unless you live in the woods, your cable comes from one of them. Almost none of the big companies anticipate skip tracers.

Some phone and Internet companies are so nice that they'll e-mail your account password to a random address if you "forget" it. My partners and I used one of these companies to access the cell phone records of a major TV celebrity we'll call the Fat Man. I don't want to use his name—despite this guy's mild demeanor on camera, he really spooked me. I was convinced my luck was going to run out if he ever discovered who had hacked his accounts.

A client called and asked us to obtain records for all four of the Fat Man's cell phones; his celebrity wife thought he was cheating on her. All of his phones were affiliated with the same customer-friendly carrier. We realized that we could easily access his accounts over e-mail, but he would receive a text message notification every time we did. That meant we only had one shot at the records. He'd know someone was trying to access his account after that.

I thought it would be best to extract the bills at three in the morning while the Fat Man was sleeping and would possibly not hear the text. I went online and set up some bogus e-mail addresses and changed the Fat Man's account information. If he woke up, I knew I would have a good lead time and be able to bang out a bunch of records. I got them all and sent them to my client the next day.

This was the first time I ever got lazy and pulled phone records from my home Internet account. I also forgot to use my anonymous surfing software—but who knows, those programs might not even work. Either way, I made a bad choice and made myself susceptible to counter-skip-tracing.

 Think your man is cheating on you? Try to get access to his cell phone records. If he has a mistress, chances are she's the first number he calls after he leaves the house in the morning and the last one he calls before he comes home at night.

The next day my client called me and in a low gritty voice said, "The Fat Man knows." We were on borrowed time, so we went through the cell phone bills together to find the lover. We found her name, her address, and—via a secret method that I will take to my grave—her photo. She was a college student, and wow . . . my client and I couldn't believe she was his mistress. The Fat Man's wife was beautiful, and this girl had totally been hit by the ugly stick. Several times.

A meeting was set up with the Fat Man and his lawyers and my client's client and lawyers. The Fat Man requested that heads roll and wanted to know who actually obtained the bills. I was freaked. My client, who also happened to be the toughest bastard in the investigative world, said to me, "Fuck that fat prick. I ain't saying nothing."

All of the lawyers were barking back and forth about who was going to sue whom, but my client kept staring down the Fat Man. Then he pulled the Ugly Stick's photo from his jacket pocket and slid it face down on the table to the Fat Man, who picked it up and had the surprise of his life. In a very calm manner, he said, "This meeting is over." Then he got up and walked out the door. I guess his image would have been seriously tarnished if my client went to the tabloids.

I never pulled phone or cellular records again after the Fat Man case. I think I've mentioned that you can get in deep shit for doing that kind of thing, and something inside me told me my time was running out. This was only a short time before the helicopter incident on the canal in Florida. Needless to say, it was a pretty paranoid time in my life.

I for one would never trade my peace of mind for a second career in illegal skip tracing. But that doesn't mean there aren't people still happy to break the law for the right price.

You might be feeling a little paranoid at this point. I'm not trying to ruin your day, but it's true: Unless you've taken special measures to conceal your personal information, it's probably out there ready for someone to find and use against you. If you really want to disappear, you have to have every bit as much creativity and balls as the skip tracers.

F*** YOU, KURT DUST

A buddy of mine named Kurt Dust is one of the greatest investigators around. He also has a wicked sense of humor, as do I. We like to pull pranks on each other from time to time.

When the tabloids started asking me to find celebrities' phone numbers, I thought up a great new prank for him.

This was back in the era of pagers. I had just discovered Nick Nolte's pager number, and so I sent him a page to call my friend Kurt. Then I sent another. And another. And about ten more after that. Every ten seconds his beeper was going crazy with this random, unrecognizable phone number. He was enraged by the time he called it. "Who the fuck is this?" he apparently said.

"Who the fuck is *this*?" Kurt said.

"What do you mean, who the fuck is this? This is fucking Nick Nolte. Who the fuck is *this*?" Their shouting match apparently continued for quite a while.

When Kurt wised up to the prank and called to cuss me out, I laughed. Then I did it again with Anna Nicole Smith's pager number. Kurt swore he would get me back, but I didn't listen.

A long time after that, on a spectacular sunny morning, I was sitting alone in my office in New Jersey when my phone rang. I picked it up and promptly had the shit scared out of me. A low, growling voice on the other end said, "You fucking prick, I know who you are, I know what you do, I am coming after you." I had no clue who it was.

I slammed the phone down and whirled around. The first thing I did was call Eileen and everyone else who worked for us. I told them not to come to work that day or ever again—we were going to have to find new digs. Then I urged them to stay in their homes all day and be vigilant, because I feared one or more of them would be attacked.

Next it was time to destroy the office. I grabbed a couple of trash bags, threw most of my things in them, smashed all the office computers, ran out the front door, and canceled my lease. No way was I ever coming back to that place.

Once safely in my car, I spent the entire day driving very, very slowly around the block, looking for potential predators. Where was this guy hiding? What was he going to do? I was freaking out.

My phone rang later that night. I almost didn't want to pick up, until I saw it was Kurt. He asked me if I'd liked his little phone call earlier.

"What?" I said.

"You fuckin' prick!" he said in the same low growl I'd heard earlier. Then he dissolved in laughter.

I have to admit, it was a pretty good prank.

4

TIME TO DISAPPEAR

ALL RIGHT, I THINK I'VE MADE IT CLEAR: IF SOMEONE'S DETERMINED to find you and has the time and money to do so, that person is going to lie, cheat, and steal in relentless pursuit. But you can head him off at every turn.

You're probably raring to go at this point: *OK, so how do I do it?* Let the games begin.

TIME FRAMES

If you're in a hurry to disappear, you might be wondering how long it will take to accomplish your goals according to my instructions. My answer is that it depends on your money and assets. The more you want to take with you when you disappear, the longer it's going to take (assuming you want to keep things legal, and I hope you do).

If you're trying to disappear with a lot of cash, you should allow yourself at least two to three months to prepare. If you're footloose and fancy-free—that is, poor—you can be out the door in a month.

Have you ever read that short story "The Most Dangerous Game," by Richard Connell? A man named Rainsford finds himself stranded on an island with a very gentlemanly but crazy old man, General

Zaroff, who likes to hunt human beings for sport. Before Rainsford knows it, he's racing through the jungle, the newest trophy item on the world's shittiest safari:

> *His whole idea at first was to put distance between himself and General Zaroff; and, to this end, he had plunged along, spurred on by the sharp rowers of something very like panic. Now he had got a grip on himself, had stopped, and was taking stock of himself and the situation. He saw that straight flight was futile; inevitably it would bring him face to face with the sea. He was in a picture with a frame of water, and his operations, clearly, must take place within that frame.*
>
> *"I'll give him a trail to follow," muttered Rainsford, and he struck off from the rude path he had been following into the trackless wilderness. He executed a series of intricate loops; he doubled on his trail again and again, recalling all the lore of the fox hunt, and all the dodges of the fox.[2]*

I don't want to give away the ending of the story, but let's just say Rainsford's cunning pays off. He knows what a successful disappearance is all about: being a little wily, a little deceptive; doing your best to cover the path you've taken while simultaneously creating false trails to throw off your pursuer.

Think of yourself as prey in the jungle: What are the three things you'll need to do to escape your predator? You'll need to camouflage yourself. You'll need to send your predator running off in another direction. And you'll need to find and build a safe new place to hide.

---

2 Richard Connell, "The Most Dangerous Game" (1924; The Nostalgia League, 1999), http://thenostalgialeague.com/olmag/connell-most-dangerous-game.html

That's more or less what disappearing is all about. It's a three-step process that involves what we in the field call **misinformation, disinformation,** and **reformation.**

Misinformation, n.: the act of finding all the information available about you and either removing it or altering it so that a skip tracer can't use it to find your real location.

Disinformation, n.: the act of fabricating information; creating bogus trails for a stalker, predator, or private investigator to find and follow.

Reformation, n.: the process of starting a new, more private life, leaving no clue as to your whereabouts.

Misinformation is about playing skip tracer yourself. The goal is to find every shred of information that exists about you and change or destroy it beyond recognition. If you're Rainsford in the jungle, you'll want to try to camouflage your body so that crazy General Zaroff can't see you running around in the bushes. You'll also want to destroy the trail that leads to you, wiping out your footprints.

Disinformation is about giving skip tracers the finger. It's my favorite part of disappearing and can be a real adventure. It's about setting up phone lines and bank accounts in cities all over the globe, nowhere near where you actually are. If you're a stalking victim, it's about providing utility companies and private mailbox companies and Internet sites with the contact information for a women's shelter, not your home, so any decent skip tracer who's on your trail will start to wonder about the person who's hired him. Rainsford spends hours making false trails for General Zaroff to follow, and later in the story, he builds a few traps, too. You should be following his example.

Reformation is the act of getting from point A to point B, of building a new life in the destination of your choice. Maybe you're moving offshore or out of state or across town, or maybe you've just committed to living more privately where you are. In any case, your new, invisible life will take planning and discipline. You can't lose the agility and cunning that you used to disappear.

There are many names for what lies at the end of this three-step path: life off the grid or under the radar; invisibility; safety; discretion. Here's the one that I think nails it best: freedom. It's a pretty sweet feeling.

Let's examine these steps one at a time.

MISINFORMATION

EVERYONE WHO WANTS MORE PRIVACY NEEDS TO DO A LITTLE misinforming. It's the key to hiding yourself from people determined to find you, whether you want to flee the country or just feel safer where you are. Sun Tzu, the ancient Chinese author of *The Art of War*, wrote that "if you know your enemies and know yourself, you will not be imperiled in a hundred battles." That's the thinking behind misinformation: If you know your vulnerabilities and consider what a pursuer might do to exploit them, you'll be able to take preventive action.

The next couple of chapters will tell you how to camouflage or remove your personal information from prying eyes. Your Misinformation Mission, should you choose to accept it, is simple:

 Identify and destroy everything that's out there on you.

The first step is to locate every piece of information that a skip tracer could possibly use to find you—that's the "identify" part. This includes current and past information. Then you'll have to get in touch with the people who provide that information and lie to them. Tell them they've got the wrong information on file and you want to "correct" it. Then, if you have the option to do so, delete the entire account. That's how you destroy.

The objective is to confuse, mislead, and head off anyone trying to snoop through your records. At best, a skip tracer will be stumped. At worst, he'll have to keep doing pretexts and searches to find your real location, and these searches take time and money. With any luck, whoever's paying him will eventually run out of cash or patience.

Most private investigators and skip tracers obey the law, but some I've known regularly break it. They'll start searching for you in obvious places: search engines, Internet databases, phone companies, utility companies. If they're comfortable breaking the law, they'll hit banks. Maybe they'll get a cop buddy to run a criminal background check and a motor vehicle report. From there they'll go

---

THE FLUKE FACTOR

Whenever a wild guess led me to a target, I called it "the fluke factor." One time, for instance, I was hired to hunt down some deadbeat who owed a lot of money to a lender. He had disappeared, leaving no forwarding addresses and no new phone. It seemed he had vanished into thin air. Everywhere I searched was a dead-end.

I went back to my client and asked if he knew more about the deadbeat. The only other piece of information the client could provide was that he was a sixties muscle car buff.

I started calling muscle car magazines to find out who handled their subscriptions. After I had the list of places to contact, I called each subscription company and claimed I was him and was curious if my magazine subscription was being forwarded to my new address. Ten calls in, I got a hit that showed the deadbeat's new address in Georgia.

---

to a laundry list of local businesses and service providers, hoping to find a valid account with your name on it. They'll use their imaginations to figure out where you might be hiding.

Your job is to use *your* imagination to anticipate their moves, and I'm here to help with that.

Start looking for yourself where I would start: a laptop connected to unsecured, public wireless Internet. Do not use your home Internet connection. That way, if a pursuer manages to hack into your laptop, he'll have no clue that you've anticipated his arrival.

Go to Zabasearch (www.zabasearch.com), a site also known as the skip tracer's Promised Land. It posts past information, which is gold when you're tracking a person, as people tend to return to where they have relatives and friends. Sometimes Zabasearch lists individuals' unpublished cell phone and landline numbers. Zaba is such a comprehensive search site that a lot of organizations are trying to shut it down.

 Enter your name on Zabasearch to see what comes up. First try a nationwide search, then narrow it down to your city and state.

Most of you will see a list of current and past addresses. You might even see your date of birth. You're also likely to see a list of relatives. Scary, huh?

Now click the Social Security link under the main search field. Enter your number and last name. You'll be directed to another big search site, Intelius (www.intelius.com), a public records company that sells information for background searches.

It will offer you a comprehensive report for something like $50. Buy it, using a prepaid credit card of course. If the person pursuing you is not going to cheap out when he's trying to find you, then you shouldn't either. Find out where Intelius got your information, and then see what you can do to remove it.

 Remove your name from Intelius People Search.

You're not going to be able to just order Intelius to stop giving out your information (unless you're a law enforcement or government official—Intelius makes exceptions for some people in that category. Contact Intelius to find out more). The company grabs its information from local public records offices. Since what it is doing is taking public information and just making it easier to find, it refuses to comply with removal requests unless you are under court protection or have a court order to have your public records sealed.

If you're a stalking victim or you fear for your life, you should pursue a court order. If you're not, there's no way you're going to be able to make your public records completely unsearchable. But you can at least make them harder to find. Intelius allows you to opt out of its "people search" service, which associates your name and address with particular public records about you, by faxing a note and a copy of your driver's license to (425) 974-6194.

Find out more on Intelius's official Web site at www.intelius.com/privacy-faq.php#5.

Zabasearch and Intelius are skip tracers' two favorite Web sites, but they're not the only data banks out there. That's why you need to expand your Internet search. You've probably Googled yourself for fun before—I mean, who hasn't? Now it's time to do it again, with purpose:

Go to every other online database and phone book you can find and figure out what they have on you.

Here are the ones I used most often as a skip tracer:
Google Phonebook
Yahoo! People Search
WhitePages.com
Superpages.com
Addresses.com
Anywho.com
BirthDatabase.com

Put your name into all of these. Write down the names of every site where you find your information publicly displayed. When you do this, use pen and paper, and be sure to flush what you've written once you're done with it. That way, you'll be safe if someone breaches security on your laptop and clones or extracts the information on your hard drive.

Once you've gone through the phone books and databases to see where you're listed, go back and find out how to delete this information. Unfortunately, I can't give you many specific instructions for removing your name from these pages, as their customer service regulations and procedures change all the time. But as a general rule, look for a link that says "FAQ"—usually one of the most frequently asked questions is: "How do I remove my information?" If you don't see something like that lurking around, look for a link that says "Contact" so you can send an e-mail or call their corporate offices for help. If that doesn't work, Google "Remove name from search engine" and see what comes up.

Here's one procedure that probably won't change anytime soon:

 Remove your name from Google Phonebook.

Here's what Google has to say: "Our phone and address listings are gathered by a third party provider, which collects telephone directories and other public records available elsewhere on the web. If you would like to have your telephone number completely unlisted (including from your local phone book), contact your local phone company and request to be both unlisted and unpublished."

Google directs you to fill out a form online, entering your information exactly as it appears in its phone book. Once you submit that form, your name will be permanently deleted from the phone book, and it won't be possible to add it again.

If you want to remove a business from Google Phonebook, you have to send a signed request on company letterhead to this address:

Google Phonebook Removal
1600 Amphitheatre Parkway
Mountain View, CA 94043

This will likewise be a permanent deletion.

If Google or any other site agrees to take down your information, call back to confirm the changes. Just because a customer service rep's told you he's made the changes does not mean he's actually done so. I've seen so many people screwed over by their failure to follow up—don't be one of them!

Next, we'll hit the standard search engines: Google, AltaVista, Yahoo, Ask.com, and all the others. Search for a number of different variations on your name, location, and workplace:

John A. Smith
John Smith
JA Smith
John AND Smith
"John Smith"
John Smith Washington D.C.
John Smith ARM Company

Next, run your e-mail address through the search engines, too. If it's John.Smith@fakeaddress.com, try:

John.Smith
John.Smith AT fakeaddress
(John.Smith) (fakeaddress)
John (DOT) Smith (AT) fakeaddress (DOT) com

 Create a Google Alert for all of these search terms. Google Alerts tell you every time someone posts a specific term to the Internet, and you can use the alerts to make sure no one re-adds your information after you've gone through and performed misinformation.

If you get a positive hit on any of these searches, write down the URL where the information is stored. Where did they get their information? Could it have been something you put up on a blog, guestbook, or online profile? Chances are good that you're the one who compromised yourself by putting your name out there in the world of social networking, so my next piece of advice should be obvious:

Take down all your social media sites.

Take them down as soon as you can. But before you hit "delete my account," make sure you've deleted all your photos, untagged all the photos other people took of you, and asked friends to delete all their photos of you or at least remove all links to your page. You don't want a skip tracer to find out who your friends are, because he could start exploiting them for information.

MORONS

My colleagues and I have found people as far away as Alaska, Paris, Germany, and Belize because their friends and relatives couldn't help but post Facebook photos of their buddy's great new life among the disappeared. Make sure your friends are a little more thoughtful than that. Better yet, don't be a moron yourself and keep your photographs private.

Go back to my chapter on "A Skip Tracer's Best Friends" and ask yourself if you're on any of the sites mentioned there. If so, delete immediately! We'll talk later in the book about how to social network safely if you must, but for now, I'm afraid you need to cut all your connections here.

Once you've removed your name from as many search engines, social networks, and other Web listings as possible, the really fun part of misinformation begins. Scrolling through Google listings can be a little tedious, I know—so I'm sure you'll be happy to hear that it's time to pick up the phone and lie, lie, lie.

As I've shown you in previous chapters, a skip tracer has plenty of ways to find you without using a computer at all. Here's a list of all the places a skip tracer might call when he's looking for you:

> phone companies
> cellular companies
> furniture stores
> electric companies
> gyms
> cable providers
> satellite providers
> Internet service providers
> video rental stores or online services
> dry cleaners
> magazine subscription services
> grocery and department store cards
> car rental agencies
> library card systems
> frequent-flier and bonus accounts
> associations and alumni groups
> banks
> credit card companies

Do you have accounts at any of these places? If the answer is yes, you're going to have to make some calls, tell some small fibs, and then delete your accounts, if you can. (Get used to the idea of buying your magazines from the rack and your DVDs from those $1 rental machines.) Sorry—you can't just call up and ask to cancel your account; the fibs are a necessary part of the game. Too many companies keep your information on file in case you ever want to join up again, and a really smart skip tracer might be able to find that information. Before you cancel, what you need to do is call up every company that has your information and change that information a little bit, marring the record in case a skip tracer ever gets his hands on it.

VANITY IS VULNERABILITY

Gyms and tanning parlors are two of the worst offenders when it comes to hoarding and storing your personal information. A lady friend of mine who likes to "fake bake" said her tanning parlor recently asked her to scan her fingerprint so that it could be sure no one else ever used her account. Her fingerprint! International law enforcement and most governments don't require law-abiding citizens to register their fingerprints, and yet a tanning parlor does? Something is wrong here.

Most gyms these days insist on taking a photo of you that pops up every time you scan your key card. Like the tanning parlors, they say they're taking measures to make sure no one else uses your account. I say they're making it easier for a stalker to find you.

As photo and fingerprint technology becomes ubiquitous at places like this, I suggest you avoid them altogether. Want to work out? Buy a pair of Nikes and pound the pavement. Need a tan? Lie out in the sun—or better yet, don't. Come on, people, haven't you ever heard of skin cancer?

Let's say your name is Arthur Aaronson, and you want to disappear. This is your contact information:

Arthur A. Aaronson
10 Main Street
Hamburg, NJ 05419

Contact all the companies and service providers that have your personal information and say:

ARTHUR: *Hi, my name is Arthur Aaronson, and I need to ask a few questions about my account.*

REP: *Sure, Mr. Aaronson. How can we help?*

ARTHUR: *I think you might have my name spelled incorrectly. It's E-R-I-N-S-O-N.*

REP: *Oh, let me fix that.*

Then call again a few days later. Say:

ARTHUR: *Hi, this is Arthur Erinson. I have a question about my account.*

Confirm your name change, then tell them you've changed jobs. You can change your job title if it's a specific one, but don't change your occupation—if a skip tracer finds your information, he'll sniff B.S. and stop looking for you down this avenue.

Rinse, wash, and repeat with all the other companies that have your information, but try to change your name to a different spelling every time: Arturo Aaronson, Arthur Erickson, Armond Aaronson. You need to do this because if a skip tracer figures out that you and "Arthur Erinson" (or Erickson) are the same person, he might assume that that is an alias and start looking for you under that name. Be unpredictable.

Some companies you contact, such as banks and utilities, might have your Social Security number on file. Giving them the wrong

Social Security number is illegal, and I am not telling you to break the law. But if you are being stalked and your life is in danger, you might choose to do what is necessary to stay alive. There's a Ralph Waldo Emerson quotation that I've been known to tell my clients from time to time: "Good men must not obey laws too well." You might choose to call the companies that have your Social Security number on file and say:

ARTHUR: *Hi, this is Arthur Aaronson. I have a question about my account.*

REP: *How can I help?*

ARTHUR: *I think one of the digits on my Social Security number is entered incorrectly in your system.*

REP: *Oh, let me change that.*

DID YOU KNOW?

The nine-digit Social Security number is composed of three parts. The first set of three digits is called the Area Number and reflects your location at birth (or whenever you were issued the card). The second two digits are the Group Number and are the Social Security Administration's way of breaking accounts into small groups. The final four digits are the Serial Number; each person in a group gets a number between 0001 and 9999, but not in consecutive order.

Why would breaking the law even be necessary? Well, as I explained, a great skip tracer can get any information he wants—and lots of companies have your Social Security number. When he goes after you, maybe he'll find your Social Security number quickly and then still be looking for your new number and address. There are a limited number of utility and phone companies in this country, and if he had the time to call them all and use the following pretext, he could eventually get your contact information:

SKIP TRACER: *Hi, my name is Arthur Aaronson, and I believe I owe you money from an old account.*

REP: *What is your address, Mr. Aaronson?*

SKIP TRACER: *I had a major drinking problem, so I bounced around—can I give you my Social?*

REP: *Sure, what would that be?*

. . . And from there he could pretext his way into getting your address.

Once you've changed your "basic identifiers," as we call them—your name, job, and your Social Security number, if you so choose—it'll be time to call each company back and change your mailing address and phone number. If you're a stalking or abuse victim, I suggest changing your contact information to that of a local police station, so a decent skip tracer will back off or start questioning his client.

If you're not a victim, there's no need to get the police involved. Choose a random post office box in a different town, then call up the customer service line on all the companies that have your information and ask to switch your address. Your skip tracer will spend his time trying to figure out who owns that P.O. box and will get bogged down in that dead-end. Again, be realistic so that the skip tracer doesn't smell B.S. If you live in a trailer park in Paducah, don't pick a P.O. box in Beverly Hills.

Write down all the new information you give these companies, so you don't forget how to locate your account in the future. Use a pen and paper.

The final thing you have to do is:

 Call up these companies and cancel as many accounts as you can.

Cancel your cell phone and switch to a prepaid phone. Do the same with your credit cards—switch to prepaid. Cancel your Netflix. Cancel your magazines. That way, there won't be an active link between these services and your contact information, and even if a skip tracer is brilliant and manages to find the old account records, they'll be totally incorrect anyway.

If you can't cancel an account—say it's your electricity account (you're not leaving your home, and you can't live in the dark)—you're going to have to keep track of what you've told the company about your new contact information. You'll also have to get used to calling up every month to ask how much money you owe. After all, if you've changed the address associated with your account, your bills are now going off into the wild blue yonder—and I don't suggest using online bill pay, as a skip tracer could find the IP address you're using to pay your bills and locate you from there. Paying over the phone is a cinch; just call the customer service line, ask how much you owe, and give them a prepaid credit card or send a money order.

IS THIS IDENTITY THEFT?

No. Purposefully introducing small errors in your record is not the same thing as creating a whole new account under a false name. You are not scamming or cheating anyone; you are not putting anyone else's credit information or reputation on the line. You are still operating as you—just with a couple of extra typos on your record.

I do not recommend that you ever hide yourself under a false identity unless you're in the Witness Protection Program and are doing it with the full cooperation of the U.S. government. It's too easy for the feds to spot identity theft, and the penalties for it are just not worth the risk.

Yes, all of this is complicated and a little tedious. But I for one think the privacy is worth it. If you agree with me, and you're like most Americans and haven't been cautious about giving out your personal information, you're going to have to make a lot of "misinformative" phone calls.

You're probably feeling overwhelmed right now. There are so many places where you could have left your information that you probably can't remember them all. But never fear: I'm here to jog your memory. The next chapter is about making sure you've sealed all the cracks.

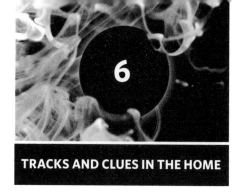

TRACKS AND CLUES IN THE HOME

METHODICAL THINKING IS THE KEY TO MISINFORMATION SUCCESS. You have to think about every place your information might be hiding, make a list, and then go deal with it. This might seem like a daunting task at first, but I find it satisfying as well, like spring cleaning or smashing a broken fax machine with a baseball bat.

The best way to figure out where you've left your personal information is to go through your house and belongings, one room at a time, and search where you might have put it. Walk with me.

YOUR WALLET AND POCKETS

Take out your wallet, open it up, and look at all those cards you have tucked away. Each of your credit cards has an amazing amount of information attached to it. Besides basic contact information and transaction records, rewards programs are probably attached to each card, too. If you get frequent-flier miles, discount rental cars, or points at a hotel chain when you charge, imagine what a skip tracer could find if he got hold of that information—especially if you'd used all those frequent-flier miles to fly off to your new life.

Do you have department store rewards cards? Frequent-buyer cards? Do these stores have your real name and contact information?

If you're walking around on a city street, you might have an iPod in your pocket, too. What does your Apple account reveal about you? Do you have an account with another online music store?

YOUR KEY RING

This is another favorite repository for customer loyalty cards. What information does your pharmacy have on you? Your grocery? What about your gym? What about the company that develops your photographs, if you still go to one of those? Did you get a free key chain or some other lame product for joining a corporate mailing list or signing up for some other promotion?

Also, as long as we're here: Who has copies of your keys? Have you ever given a copy to a significant other, friend, or cleaning lady? If you terminated the relationship with this person, did you ever get the key back? Can you be sure he or she hasn't gone out and made copies? Have you simply gotten careless about giving out copies of your keys? If so, it might be time to change your locks.

THE LIVING ROOM

Walk into your living room or family room. If you have a TV, DVD player, stereo, or any other electronic device, you have a warranty on it. What did you put on that warranty card? Do manufacturers have your current address and cell phone number? If the items were a gift, did whoever gave them to you put their or your contact information on file? Either way, a warranty is a gold mine for skip tracers and private investigators. If we don't find your contact information, we might find the address and phone number of an old friend or family member whom we can trick into sharing details about you.

The same goes for your couch, love seat, and big old ottoman. Do you have warranties on those? What would a stranger be able to find out if he pretended to be you and talked to the people who sold you this stuff?

How did you pay for all of these things? With a credit card or through a store account? Any smart skip tracer or stalker who's on your trail would be able to obtain your credit report and locate the furniture store, the rug company, or the Best Buy where you went shopping. Then the skip tracer could contact the store and say he's you, say he can't locate the warranty information on the sixty-inch— or whatever you bought. Five minutes later, he has your address and phone number on a piece of paper.

If you think all of this is a little extreme—that someone trying to find you would never go this far—think again. I've used warranties and charge cards to find people all over the globe.

THE BATHROOM

This is a dangerous place, even if you've never slipped in the shower. Your medicine cabinet is loaded with private information. Drug labels identify your condition and list your doctor and pharmacy. The pharmacy has a record of your medical insurer, who has a lovely list of all your medical issues.

Let's say you're a politician or another public figure. You probably don't want anyone to know that you're on Prozac or Xanax or, God forbid, Viagra, but people who want to harm you will try to find out. Just ask the Republican operative who hired me in the early nineties to find out if then-Governor Bill Clinton had ever been admitted to a mental hospital in Arkansas. (He hadn't.)

THE GARAGE

This is a skip tracer's paradise. We can find your whereabouts using anything from the lawn mower, the weed whacker, the lawn trimmer, and the electric hedge clippers down to forgotten old junk stored in boxes. Most of these items have serial numbers on them, and those serial numbers are attached to warranties and purchases. The warranties are attached to purchase orders, which probably have your name, address, phone number—and whatever other information you gave out—all over them.

You can't be sure that someone's not going to use your stuff to steal your identity unless you've removed the serial numbers from everything you own—especially before you dispose of it or sell it at a garage sale.

People also tend to use the garage as limbo land. It's where you put boxes of things you're not sure what to do with: old papers, college books, bank records, love letters, pool toys. The problem is that when people decide to chuck the box, they'll do a quick scan,

---

WHAT'S THE DEAL WITH DOCTORS?

Unfortunately, medicine is a crucial part of all of our lives, and we all have to participate in the health care system. But as someone who takes his privacy seriously, I find doctors' offices very frustrating. When you go to new doctors, you're always given a privacy information sheet assuring you that they're required by law to keep your information confidential. But then as soon as you're done reading, they want to make a copy of your driver's license and write down your Social Security number.

Why do doctors need to know? I understand that they need to make sure they get paid for their services, but if you're paying with an insurance card, shouldn't that be enough? They can always go harass the insurance company, and then the insurance company can come harass you.

If you don't want to divulge any personal information on a form, leave it blank. You are not legally required to give your doctor your Social Security number unless you are on Medicare or Medicaid.[1] Same goes for your pharmacy.

---

1 Barbara Kiviat, "Guarding Your Social Security Number," *Time*, Deember 4, 2007, http://www.time.com/time/business/article/0,8599,1690827,00.html

not really searching through what's inside. Take the time to *search* the boxes.

A client made a big mistake when he and his wife put some compromising videos out on the street corner in a garbage bag. Were they picked up by the garbage truck and destroyed, or are they on the Internet now, thanks to some creepy trash man? Their problem is that they won't know if the videos are buried deep in a landfill or offered as free content on a porn site.

THE BEDROOM

Speaking of sex tapes, just keep this area private.

THE KITCHEN

There are probably lots of warranties on the items in here—on your refrigerator, your microwave, your stove—but the food you're cooking inside those appliances could get you, too. Where do you buy your food? Are you in some kind of price club or food co-op? Almost all of these stores offer "affinity" cards that you have to scan at the register in order to get the sale price on the weekly specials. These stores have your address and phone number on file, and some even have your checking account information. And of course they know what you buy, where you buy it, and when. Why did you give these people real information?

Are you a foodie? Do you subscribe to any food magazines or get deliveries from any specialty food companies? A clever skip tracer will use this information to find you. One time I was searching for a guy in the Midwest. For the life of me, everywhere I looked I came up empty-handed. I went back to the woman who had hired me to find him and asked if she could tell me anything more. She could only remember one more thing: He ate a lot of lobster.

I decided to search companies that shipped lobsters. I called a bunch of seafood delivery companies, and one company finally brought up his name. To confirm the account, they matched his name with his prior address. Imagine: located because of lobster love. It was so simple.

THE HOME OFFICE

Your computer and where you keep it are probably the most vulnerable places in your house. Your IP address and the information on your hard drive will tell an intruder or a hacker everything he needs to know to find you or to steal your identity. If a skip tracer or stalker can get his hands on your computer or the information you're sending over an unprotected wireless connection that you've installed in your home, he'll instantaneously know where you are, where you're headed, and what you plan to do when you get there. (Activity on an unsecured wireless connection in a public place is harder to trace: There are dozens of people using it at any given time and there's no way to identify a particular user unless you know his IP address.)

Even if you backed over it with your truck on the way out the door, your computer's hard drive could tell all to someone determined to find you. And your printer and scanner are even worse. I've heard that

---

NOT RECOMMENDED: ANONYMIZING SOFTWARE

In the past, I told clients to make their home computers safe by buying software that makes their Web activity anonymous. But I stopped recommending that when I realized I had no clue whether that stuff actually worked. Here's the safest way to protect your Web activity: Don't ever do sensitive or incriminating stuff on your home computer.

---

when you print something, there is an identifier that can match printed paper to an individual printer. Manufacturers don't publicize this—yet another example of big business equaling Big Brother. I'm sure it won't be long until printers and scanners secretly copy every item printed and scanned, and hold this information for somebody like me to find.

Most people keep their bills and files next to their computers in their home office. If you shred these, you shouldn't throw the shreds in the trash can—someone who's really determined might be able to put them back together. You should be flushing that stuff . . . but then again, in the age of customer-friendly, low-security utility companies, maybe it's not even worth the trouble.

DO I REALLY NEED TO DO THIS?

If you're just reading this book for fun, I know what you're thinking: Why go to all this trouble if I'm not on the run? You pay your bills, no one is stalking you, and what do you have to worry about?

You're right—you probably don't have to worry. But plenty of innocent, law-abiding men and women get their identities stolen every year. Remember what I told you: Your personal information is a valuable commodity, no matter who you are. Corporations buy and sell personal data every day, and plenty of individuals do, too. The more you know about your vulnerabilities, the better.

FINAL THOUGHTS

If you've gone through your house, made a note of your vulnerabilities, and called up and misinformed every single manufacturer and service provider who has your information, congratulations. You're almost ready to move on.

Before you do, though, I highly recommend that you double-check your work by hiring a private investigator to try to find you. That way, you can be sure you've sealed all the cracks. Don't pay the PI with a credit card. Send him cash or a money order. And pick a PI who's far, far away—nowhere near your home state. You never know who's been hired to find you around where you live.

Give him your name and one other basic identifier—such as a past address or phone number—and see how much dirt he can dig up about you. This is how my partner Eileen and I used to check up on each other's work.

If he turns up any information, see if any of it will lead to your current location. Patch up whatever holes you can, and then get ready to step up your game for phase two: disinformation.

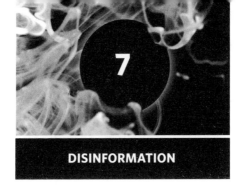

DISINFORMATION

DISINFORMATION IS MY FAVORITE PART OF DISAPPEARING, BECAUSE it brings my skip tracer's talent for deception into play.

In the first step of your disappearing act, misinformation, you took what was out there on you and hid it from view. Now you're going to make finding you even more difficult by creating a bunch of bogus trails for your pursuer to follow. You'll do this with two goals in mind:

 Keep your hunter busy searching for you in the wrong place, and make the file on you as thick, frustrating, and expensive to detangle as possible.

When I was a skip tracer, my buddies and I prayed we'd get just enough information to find our targets—no more, no less. Too little information and the trail would go cold, but too much and we couldn't tell the bogus trails from the real ones.

When people pick up and disappear, one common and crucial mistake they make is that they do not attempt to keep their hunters busy. If you just leave one trail, however hard you've tried to cover it, you allow your pursuer the opportunity to search it thoroughly. Don't give him that luxury. Skip tracers are some of the quickest and most imaginative people you'll meet, if I do say so myself, and if they're on the right trail, they'll probably find you.

Therefore, it is very important that you do some disinformation. Think of it as con artistry in the name of self-defense. Like any good con, it consists of three parts: **hook, line,** and **sinker.**

THE HOOK

Your "hook" is a piece of information you create on purpose for a hunter to find. It looks real and will excite a skip tracer when he finds it. Perhaps you'll express interest in a home loan or an apartment rental or a credit card, causing someone to run an inquiry on your credit report. Perhaps you'll make calls from a phone line you know your pursuer will access.

Hooks are a great tool for victims of stalking and abuse. I once worked with a client named Vera, whose husband, the father of her child, had beaten and threatened to kill her. He was graduating from a three-year stint in the gray bar motel, and even from prison he had attempted to terrorize her by sending anonymous, threatening letters. When his release date was nearing, he made it obvious that he was planning to come back and hurt her.

Vera had full custody of their child and wasn't about to let that happen. She wanted to get the hell out of her hometown, so she got in touch with me. After we did some misinformation on her record, we created a realistic and elaborate disinformation plan that would keep her ex busy and off her trail.

The first thing Vera and I did was send her off to a small town in the Midwest and locate an apartment for rent. We made sure that the apartment complex would run a credit check, creating an inquiry on her credit report. We suspected the jailbird ex would persuade someone to run a credit report on her, and we knew he or an investigator would notice that inquiry from Sincere Realty in Buck, Oklahoma. That inquiry was our **hook.**

THE LINE
Vera and I knew that the minute the jailbird read the inquiry, he would be on a bus across the country, heading straight for Buck. So we created a **line:** a whole mess of information in that location. We had Vera apply for utilities and phone service for the apartment she visited—even though she was not moving in, nor would she be there to activate the services.

We assumed the jailbird would hire a skip tracer or private investigator to help him find an apartment number. If a professional were on Vera's trail, he would locate an incomplete order for telephone service at her new "address"—possibly a complete order, if a new tenant moved into the apartment. He'd be confused: Did Vera not take the apartment, or did she move in with a roommate? And he'd have to go there to investigate, costing the jailbird more money and time.

The telephone company from which Vera applied for phone service asked for employment information and a contact phone number. We located a large company that was in the area and used that as her employment address. Then we used a contact phone for the same company—but at another location, in a different city. We hoped that the ex and his hired goon would think she had transferred locations, and yet another dead-end search would begin.

Team Jailbird could pretext and skip-trace all over Oklahoma—they would never find Vera. When they didn't find her name in utility accounts, perhaps they'd try the phone company, the cable TV company, and local grocery stores. Each of these searches was going to cost money—racking up an investigative bill in the hundreds, if not the thousands—and each would take time.

THE SINKER

Before Vera hit the road to her new, undisclosed location, we opened up a small checking account at a random bank. She called this bank from her old phone and her mother's, along with a few other banks for good measure. Then she asked for a debit card, which I passed along to an associate of mine who travels all over the country. Soon, "Vera" was going shopping in St. Louis, Montreal, Seattle . . . you name it.

That was our **sinker:** a clue so wild that it would take a private investigator *years* to get her head around it. If Team Jailbird managed to acquire either set of phone records, they'd see bank numbers and think they'd hit the start of Vera's money trail. Perhaps the private investigator would call the banks and make the very illegal move of pretending to be Vera. She'd find an active account at one of the places she called and think, bingo. We've got her now.

Then she'd extract withdrawal records and see the following:

ATM $20.00 St. Louis, MO
ATM $30.00 Chicago, IL
ATM $10.00 Las Vegas, NV
ATM $20.00 Toronto, ONT
ATM $40.00 Montreal, QC
ATM $10.00 Seattle, WA

She'd think, my God, this woman is on the move. She might even do some preliminary investigating in these cities, wasting even more time and money. Even if the jailbird had limitless resources, the PI might be so frustrated at this point that she gives up.

If your life is in danger, there's not much to enjoy about disappearing, but it's hard not to feel satisfied when a plan like this works. Vera is still safe today, and you know what? We enjoyed giving her jailbird the finger. Fuck him!

No matter how much stress you're under as you try to disappear, I hope you can step back and appreciate your creative finesse as you confuse the hell out of your pursuers. The truth is: Disinformation can be fun. If you don't believe me, let me introduce you to another client: Louie, one of my all-time favorites.

LOUIE

When Louie first came to see me, he reminded me of a chubby, foul-mouthed George Peppard—you know, that guy who was on *The A-Team* back in the eighties. (Sorry, I like my classic TV.) He was from Brooklyn, and he came into my office sucking smoke from a foot-long Cuban cigar. He told me he'd made a fortune running hot dog carts and lunch wagons, and now his bottom-feeding son was trying to take his money. The son was a lawyer—an ambulance chaser—and he wanted to get power of attorney over his father so that he could take a bite out of the hot dog assets.

Louie wasn't about to let that happen. He was a widower, but he was far from senile or incapable of managing his affairs. He wanted his son off his back, and he knew the best way to do that would be to disappear. Move to the Caribbean. Enjoy his fortune and a cold Corona next to a bright blue sea.

My first move was to locate an escort in Miami and explain that I had a client who was interested in putting her up in a place and paying all of her living expenses. The escort was more than happy to indulge. I located an apartment in a building with a doorman and had Louie rent the place and set up cable, utilities, and a phone line in his name. A short time after that, the escort moved in and made herself at home.

A few weeks later, Louie was relaxing on a Caribbean beach, and we started our disinformation campaign. I had a Miami relocation packet sent to Louie's old place; we had purposefully refrained from starting mail forwarding at that place. We knew the son was grabbing the mail, so we figured he would start searching in Miami.

We assumed Louie's son would hire a private investigator. I knew that the first thing one of my colleagues would do was contact the utility company to search for services. In no time, he could extract Louie's address and phone number using the simple pretext of: "Hi, this is Louie Hotdog, and I may owe you money on my bill—can you check for me?"

The private investigator would forward that contact information to Louie's son, and if he called the number, he'd get the gruff voice of Louie saying, "Leave a message." Eventually, the son would tire of his unreturned calls and contact a private investigator in the area to go to the apartment.

Guess what? Our predictions came true, big time. The son hired a private investigator who sat surveillance in front of the building. He never saw Louie come or go. Eventually, he made his way to the doorman and flashed a photo of Louie, but the doorman said he'd never seen such a person come or go. He insisted that Louie did not live in the building.

Louie and I believe that the private investigator coughed up some cash to the doorman and learned that the escort was living in Louie's apartment. The investigator confronted the escort, who was kind enough to let him know that Louie was simply a generous client who supported her. She also admitted that she had never met Louie; she gave him a contact phone number.

The phone number was smack in the middle of Florida. When the son called it, it rang and rang—and then he heard his own voice. It was his own home voice-mail machine. We had had the phone company install a construction line on a rural piece of property, and we used a remote call-forwarding service to program the son's home phone number. Anyone who dialed "Louie's" phone number would get the son's house on Long Island.

Hook, line, and what a sinker. Boy, was that son pissed. He dropped the search.

YEP—DISINFORMATION CERTAINLY CAN BE SATISFYING. BUT YOU CAN learn other lessons from this story. You might be in a totally different situation from Louie's, but if you want to disappear as successfully as he did, you need to adopt a few of the same principles:

 Don't be cheap. What's more important, your cash or your privacy?

Louie was willing to splash out on an elaborate plan to distract his son. You might not have the money to rent an apartment and hire an escort to live there, but do whatever you can. Open a small checking account and give the ATM card to a traveling friend. Fly out to some random city to look at apartments and meet real estate agents, and have them run a credit check. Make some long-distance phone calls to banks and employers in another city.

 **Be creative.**

Louie's plan had a lot of panache, and so should yours. Maybe you've decided to create a trail of false leads in Atlanta, Georgia. Really take the time to think about the cleverest thing a pursuer could do to try to find you. Then go do it. Think of it as performance art!

Like celebrities? Send *In Touch Weekly* to an apartment you've scoped out. (You'll make the tenant's day.) Fruit fanatic? Order a big old box of peaches from Dickey Farms and send it in your name to some random workplace. Take a tour of CNN studios and send the pictures back to your old house. Go to the Coca-Cola factory and sign the guestbook. The harder a skip tracer feels he's had to work for a nugget of information, the more convinced he'll be that it's a real lead. He'll think he's the smartest guy in the world when he finds your clues.

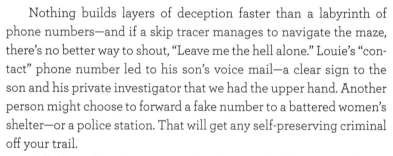

Call-forwarding services are your best friend.

Nothing builds layers of deception faster than a labyrinth of phone numbers—and if a skip tracer manages to navigate the maze, there's no better way to shout, "Leave me the hell alone." Louie's "contact" phone number led to his son's voice mail—a clear sign to the son and his private investigator that we had the upper hand. Another person might choose to forward a fake number to a battered women's shelter—or a police station. That will get any self-preserving criminal off your trail.

Call forwarding is a great tool, and as you finish up your deception campaign and get ready to make a run for it, a lot of other tools will help you disappear without a trace. So before we move to stage three of the disappearing process—reformation—I want to arm you to the teeth with all the weapons you need for a clean getaway.

YOUR REFORMATION ARSENAL

CONGRATULATIONS. YOU'RE ALMOST READY FOR THE MOMENT when all your hard work pays off: Disappearing Day. Now that you've covered your trail and sent your pursuers on a wild-goose chase, it's time to load up on everything you need to start building your new life. Used in the right way, these simple tools will help you complete a successful **reformation:** a new, private life in the location of your choice.

Here's what you need to pull this off.

PREPAID CREDIT CARDS

Go to your local convenience store or Walmart *today* and pick up some prepaid credit cards. They are your new best friends. Use prepaid credit cards, gift cards, or cash to buy everything else in this chapter. If you're serious about disappearing, stop using your other credit cards immediately. Credit card records are just too easy to extract.

 If you are married and looking to get divorced and you do not want your spouse to know you're stashing money away for the big move, use cash to buy prepaid credit cards and gift cards from local stores. So many places offer gift cards, and the best part is that none of this shows up on your credit. Stash all of your prepaid cards in your Main Drop Box (see "How to Use Mail Drops" below).

PREPAID PHONES AND CALLING CARDS

Say good-bye to your old cell phone. It's one of your biggest vulner-abilities, as I hope the previous couple of chapters showed. Don't just throw it out—stomp it into as many pieces as you can and throw them in several public trash cans.

Since phone companies are so easy to pretext, it's vital that you learn to communicate with prepaid phones, which are available from pretty much any wireless store. You're going to need to change these frequently—very frequently if you're making a lot of phone calls.

Don't get lazy or tightfisted about this, and give out as little personal information as possible when you're registering the phone. Whenever you buy a prepaid cell phone, "accidentally" misspell your name if you are required to register the phone, and make your address as hard to read as possible. Pay with a prepaid credit card or in cash. If you run out of credit, avoid topping up online; go to a local convenience store, and again—pay in cash.

Prepaid phones are not a foolproof way to communicate. You should think of them as slightly safer than a standard cell phone or landline, but not 100 percent secure. The only untraceable part of the phone is the name of the owner, provided, of course, that you gave the phone company a not-quite-correct name (which you did, didn't you?!). Everything else, including the calls you make and the approximate area you make them from, is traceable.

My partner Eileen worked a murder case in which the defendant claimed to be using his prepaid cell phone in an area far from the crime scene. One of the defense attorneys on the case subpoenaed the cellular records from the prepaid company for Eileen to review, and to our amazement, the records from the cell towers showed us at what speed and in which direction the client was moving. This information didn't come from a GPS receiver; it came from the cell towers. Removing the GPS device from your phone is not going to make you untraceable.

Before you start having a panic attack, let me assure you that it would be *very* hard to trace a prepaid cell phone based on this kind of cell tower information. I doubt it's available to customer service representatives. Without a subpoena, I'm not sure a skip tracer could get it. But I believe that any information can be obtained for the right price, so be careful.

USING PREPAID PHONES AND CALLING CARDS TO TALK TO LOVED ONES

Let's say the only people you want to stay in contact with after you disappear are your mother and your sister. Maybe you have a crazy ex with tons of money, strong contacts in the world of skip tracers and private investigators, and a determination to hunt you down. You have to communicate with caution, so the rotten SOB doesn't locate you and chop you up into a million pieces.

Buy a prepaid phone and make a note of the number. We'll call it the Break Phone. Load it up with a few thousand minutes, paying in cash. Ask your mother to get a prepaid phone, too. That way, you don't have to make a call to her home number or her billed cell phone. To find you, your stalker would have to intercept a prepay-to-prepay call, and he'd have to have some Homeland Security–style equipment to do that.

Make sure you get an owner's manual with your Break Phone. Then take a long drive, consult the owner's manual for how to set up the call-forwarding feature, and program the phone to forward to your mother's.

Then: smash! Take the battery out, stomp on the Break Phone, and dump it. Go back to a different wireless store, buy a different

Break Phone, and repeat the above, programming it to forward to your sister's number.

Now you need to buy a third phone and a prepaid calling card— from a third wireless store, preferably after a long drive. Buy a fresh prepaid phone and calling card. From the Fresh Phone, use the prepaid calling card to call the prepaid Break Phone belonging to your mother or your sister—whomever you're trying to reach. She will answer, and you can have your conversation.

When you are done with the Fresh Phone, erase the call from your calling history—simple to do in the "options" menu on most phones—and dump the phone on the street. Leave the calling card in a different location near a coin phone.

REMINDER

When you delete a call from your calling history, you've deleted it from the *phone,* not the phone company's records. That's why it's so important that you change your phones frequently: Your phone records are still out there for a skip tracer to find.

Eventually, someone will pick up the Fresh Phone and the calling card and use them. If the call to your mother is traced, it will first be traced to the toll-free number of the prepaid calling card. Then it will go to the Break Phone. From the Break Phone a skip tracer will have to locate the incoming calls to locate the Fresh Phone, which is now being used by someone roaming the streets. It's a great diversion.

It's possible that whoever locates your Break Phone number might deactivate the call-forwarding function, but that won't matter—just start the process over again.

If you do all this, are you communicating in a completely safe way? No. But you have created layers in your communications, and most likely, a skip tracer or stalker will not be able to track you down. Every time you buy a different phone from a different carrier, finding your information will take one more costly and time-consuming pretext.

Some of you might be thinking, "What about law enforcement?" Of course they can pierce this structure. They have the technology and the subpoena power. That's why you don't want to break the law.

MORON

I was recently asked to provide a comment for a magazine article about a man named Matthew Alan Sheppard, who tried to fake his own death by "drowning" in a river and then sneaking off to Mexico. He used a tactic I mention here: He left his BlackBerry in a gas station so that anyone who suspected he was still alive would look at the cell records and follow them straight to a bum on the street. *That doesn't work if it's a phone registered in your name.*

A bum actually did pick up the phone, used it a few times, and dumped it. Acting on a hunch, a detective looked at Sheppard's cell phone records, saw that text messages had been sent after Sheppard supposedly drowned, and was immediately convinced that Sheppard was the one who sent them. The hunt began.

Sheppard went to prison.

VIRTUAL PHONE NUMBERS

If all this mess with prepaid phones sounds like more trouble than it's worth, you can buy a virtual number that has no physical location.

You can get one from JConnect (www.jconnect.com). These numbers let you collect voice mail delivered to the e-mail of your choice. You can get faxes on JConnect, too, or via Efax (www.efax.com).

These numbers are a great tool: You can set them up online and in a hurry. They're not too expensive, either. Right now, a phone line on JConnect costs $19.95 a month—and you can purchase a phone number anywhere in the world. Want to convince someone you're in Paris? No problem—just buy a local Paris phone number and leak it to your pursuer through disinformation. Need a safe way for your family to call you without worrying about your safety or their long distance fees? Buy a phone number from a nearby area code that doesn't charge long distance. The possibilities are endless.

MAIL DROPS

If you don't want someone to know where you live or where you're headed, you're going to need an anonymous place to receive mail. Actually, you're going to need several. As with prepaid phones, it's best that you create a complex system involving multiple drops. That way a stalker on your trail can't untangle the mess if he manages to acquire your records from a particular mail drop.

Go to a UPS Store or some other private mailbox store and buy one of its boxes. You're going to have to provide ID: That's OK. This is only the first of several mailboxes you're going to buy, and ultimately it's going to be hard for a skip tracer to get to you. We'll refer to this box as your Main Drop.

When you open the Main Drop, pay in advance with a prepaid credit card. A year's worth of payment is best. Explain to the owner of the drop that you travel extensively and want to be able to have your mail shipped to different locations and you would like to leave X amount of dollars on account for future shipping. Leave as much as possible.

TIP: DON'T USE A P.O. BOX

Don't open a mailbox at a post office. The U.S. Postal Service is an easy place to obtain information. Most people who have or had P.O. boxes have resided in that zip code. So if a skip tracer is searching for you and somehow stumbles on your P.O. box, he would go to any online search company and run your name with the city, and most likely a history of addresses in that locale will follow. A good skip tracer could run your name or identifiers from there, using the phone, utility, or cable TV company to locate a current or closed account.

In my twenty years on the job, I've located almost every deadbeat who's tried to shield himself behind a P.O. box. But in all those years, I haven't been able to pretext a privately owned mail drop.

If you're about to leave the state or the country, use this Main Drop to store documents, your prepaid phone, your prepaid credit cards, your new lease, and bank statements from your new accounts. Every time you buy something you intend to use when you disappear, mail those items to your Main Drop. Use bogus return addresses from all over the globe when you send things to yourself. Don't be worried that the postmarks will give you away when you use these bogus addresses. Nobody notices. Just make sure to use the correct postage!

Now, from an Internet cafe, search online for another mail drop. Secure this one from an e-mail address you set up specifically for this purpose—you should be setting up a new e-mail address for every mail drop you buy. We'll call this new box your Burn Box.

When you've located a suitable Burn Box, buy another prepaid credit card and load it with enough money to pay for a few months for the Burn Box (how many exactly depends on how much mail you're going to need to receive before you relocate). Use separate prepaid credit cards for every mail drop you buy. If you have money left over on the prepaid credit card after paying for the Burn Box, I suggest dropping the credit card in a mall or on the bus or in a store, letting some stranger use the card elsewhere, creating a false trail. I'd also tell you to wipe the card of prints . . . but I know you're not breaking the law.

When you are filling out the information for the Burn Box, you may be asked for a phone number. Give them a JConnect or other virtual phone number if you can. For an e-mail address, give them the designated e-mail you chose for that Burn Box. Give them the

---

STORE YOUR VITALS THE SAFE WAY

- Go online—*not* using your home connection—and post information about your location on a message board, a free classified ad site, or a blog you've just created via a free, anonymous blog service. Post or create a blog using an e-mail address you've created specifically for this purpose.

- Post your information in a way you'll recognize, but disguise the details. For instance, if you have a mailbox at 642 Fake Street, Orlando, Florida, you could post "Women's shoes, size 6, and matching skirt, Euro size 42. Fake designer. Ships from Orlando" on a free classified ad site.

- Use several sites and several e-mail addresses to store your information. You can never be too safe! But the Internet is so huge that it will be easy to hide your information in plain sight.

- Remember: Always keep track of your information locations in a notebook and keep that notebook with you at all times.

---

address to your Main Drop; do not write clearly, and perhaps make a typo. Make a one look like a seven and a four look like a nine, so that if a skip tracer happens to get this far on your trail, he'll be confused.

Keep track of all the information about this box and all your other mailboxes, but don't store it on a computer hard drive.

Now it's time to open two other mailboxes in two other locations—locations that are as far apart from each other as you can feasibly drive. We'll call these your Safe Box and your Bluff Box. You will now have four mailboxes: the Main Drop, the Burn Box, the Safe Box, and the Bluff Box. Why you need all four will become clear in the next section.

HOW TO USE MAIL DROPS

As you prepare to disappear, you're going to be acquiring lots of information, including contracts, guidebooks, forms, and paperwork for an anonymous corporation you might decide to create (I'll explain later in this chapter). The information you receive will fall into two categories: information you *need* from the place you want to move to, and information you can *dump* because it's coming from places where you performed disinformation (real estate material, bank statements, etc.).

You're going to have to tell these two categories apart as you send them to your Main Drop, so use a different but specific fake return address for each. For instance, you could give all the information in your *need* category a return address in Cincinnati and all the information in your *dump* category a return address in Baltimore.

When it's time to hit the road, you can acquire the information you need safely by calling up the people who provide your Main Drop and giving them specific instructions:

1. Have your Cincinnati return address mail packed in one over-night package to your Bluff Box.

2. Your Baltimore return address packages are your dump mail, so have them sent via regular mail to the Bluff Box as well.

3. As you wait for these packages, thicken the plot for whoever manages to pretext your Main Drop by sending as many real estate pamphlets, utility applications, and relocation kits as possible to the Main Drop—using your Bluff Box as the return address. The more disinformation, the better! You want to make sure a skip tracer doesn't know whether anything coming into or out of that Main Drop is a credible lead.

4. Once your Cincinnati information arrives in the Bluff Box, have the Bluff Box's providers ship that box to the Burn Box, and from the Burn Box, ship it to the Safe Box. Then cancel your Burn Box.

5. Once the Baltimore information arrives in the Bluff Box, you can destroy it. Then let your Bluff Box expire and do not renew.

As I said, I've never had any luck extracting information from a privately owned mail drop. But that doesn't mean no one will. You just never know, and that's why I recommend you follow this proto-col. Consider it another step in your disinformation campaign: It will confuse and frustrate your pursuers. I bet it took you a few readings to understand, too.

CORPORATIONS

I highly recommend you establish a corporation and transfer your lease, car loan, utilities, and whatever else is legally possible to its name. If people are hunting you down and your house and services are in the name of Frank's Disappearing World Inc., they are going to have a real problem connecting these things to you.

I would offer specific advice about the state or country where you should open up your corporation, but everyone's needs are different and laws about these things change quickly. So instead of providing you with information that will be archaic in six months, I'll give you some keywords for conducting online research about corporations and companies that can help you incorporate (see sidebar).

KEYWORDS FOR BUILDING YOUR CORPORATION

"Anonymous Corporations"

"Shelf Corporations"

"Nominee Corporations"

"Delaware Corporations"

"Offshore Corporations"

"Nevada Corporations"

"International Business Corporations"

Search these terms thoroughly online to find out what type of corporation is right for you. Whether you want to open one in Nevada or Wyoming or Delaware or somewhere offshore like Guatemala depends on whether you intend to leave the country and where you intend to live.

Either way, before you buy, you're going to need to set up the mail drop system I just described. That way, you can have a secure address to send your corporation paperwork and you won't have to worry about it being discovered if someone robs your house or hacks your computer.

Incorporating is not as pricey as you think. You can start a corporation for a couple of hundred dollars on a site like LegalZoom.com or TheNevadaCompany.com.

COMPUTERS, E-MAIL, AND E-MAIL ADDRESSES

If you can, buy a new computer. But keep using your old computer and home Internet connection for nonsecure tasks so that anyone who discovers your IP address or hacks into your hard drive will think he's on to you. Why not do some disinformation while you're at it? Look up a few random exotic locations and apartment complexes from your home Internet, creating more expensive and time-consuming dead-ends for your pursuer to find.

If you do manage to buy a new computer, *never* use it to access the Internet from your home. Drive a few miles from your house and look for unsecured, free, public wireless Internet (New Yorkers: Did you know it's available in Times Square now?). Do this even if you just want to look at something stupid like DailyPuppy.com. The point is that you don't want anyone to associate your name with this IP address, so later on you can use it to monitor your JConnect and mail drop accounts.

If you can't afford a new computer, use an Internet cafe to do your online chores. *Never* print anything when you're at a cafe, as cafe printers log what you print and when. Remember that most Internet cafes have security cameras these days. Also, many people have been robbed or hacked after using a public terminal because, unbeknownst to them, a criminal had installed key-capture software on the unit and captured their log-ins and passwords.

As for what you do when you're on the computer: You might have noticed that I am a big proponent of using lots of different e-mail addresses. The more anonymous Hushmail, Gmail, and

Yahoo addresses you use to conduct your business, the safer you are. Needless to say, don't create an e-mail address that offers clues to your identity, such as HarleyFan15 if you're a motorcycle junkie. Better yet, get an e-mail address that looks as if it couldn't possibly be yours: If you are in the States, get a British or French address. (And like everything else you'll want to do while creating your new life, keep a notebook of all your own information—e-mail addresses, P.O. boxes, cell phone numbers, special accounts, etc.; it's easy to lose your way.)

I am not a technology expert, but I know how to err on the side of safety, and that's by staying anonymous. You won't have to worry about anyone getting your credit card or Social Security number from an unsecured wireless connection if you never give either of those numbers out online, and that's what I'm advocating you do. But if you're still worried about staying safe, I would consult any of the number of fine books on personal Internet safety already available (in a bookstore cafe, of course, or after paying in cash).

BOOKS AND BOOKSTORES

Remember my story about how I got into the disappearing business? I watched a guy in a bookstore buy J. J. Luna's *How to Be Invisible*, guides to Costa Rica, and offshore travel books . . . with a credit card. Rookie mistake. The more you can read up on how to disappear, the better, but *do not pay with your credit card.*

It's best if you don't pay for books at all. No, I'm not recommending you steal—just that you use the bookstore as a library. Keep in mind that with cameras in wider use than ever, it is nearly impossible to buy something in a store without being recorded. So, your safest bet is to head to the bookstore cafe with a big stack of books and a notepad. Flush the notes you no longer need when you're done with them, and send the ones you do need to your Main Drop box.

If you have any bookstore membership, or belong to a book club, lending library, or any type of entity that has kept track of books you purchased or read, you need to perform misinformation on that account. Use an Internet people search to find someone else who has the same first name as you, then call up the bookstore and say that you've moved, providing the other person's address. If no one else has your name, find someone with a similar first name (a Ron if you're a Rob) and call the bookstore up to say it has your name wrong *and* you've moved.

If your credit card is attached to the account, call up and remove your credit card information. Delete all stored credit cards and addresses from your accounts with online retailers like Amazon and AbeBooks.

It is important that you find out exactly what information bookstores have about you: your contact number, e-mail address, etc. Make sure they change the information they have, and call back to confirm that they have no record of the older information. Call back to confirm yet again if you have extra time and want to be doubly sure.

FRANK'S PHILOSOPHY

When things are changed twice, it's nice, but three can set you free.

If they have your e-mail address on file, make sure you change that, too. But don't give them a bogus address—give them a new one that you've created just for this. (Why? If an e-mail address in a company's system bounces back, that address will be kicked out of the system, which will then most likely restore your original e-mail address.)

READING LIST

There's only one other book on personal privacy that I recommend you read on your jaunt to the bookstore: J. J. Luna's *How to Be Invisible.* Depending on where you're going and what you plan to do, look for the latest offshore banking guides and travel books about the place you want to move. Mix a couple of totally irrelevant how-to books and travel guides into your pile, too, and look around for cameras before you sit down. You never know who's watching.

OTHER TOOLS YOU MIGHT NEED

Ultimately, what you're going to need for a successful life off the radar depends on where you live, what you're doing, and how you intend to support yourself. Everyone will need prepaid phones and calling cards. Some might benefit from the following tools as well:

- A **spoof card,** which offers the ability to change what people see on their caller ID when you phone them. You can find these pretty easily by entering "spoof card" in Google.
- **Alibi services,** which offer bogus alibis from travel agencies, hotels, seminars, and "employers." These also offer rescue calls for bad dates. The most famous company, Alibi Network (www.alibinetwork.com), has been featured on ABC News's *Nightline,* the *Today* show, and elsewhere, but an Internet search will reveal dozens more.
- **Discreet voice mail services,** which allow you to log in and send a voice mail that will go straight to a person's mailbox without ringing her phone.

NOT RECOMMENDED: CAMOUFLAGE PASSPORTS

As you prepare to disappear, you might come across Web sites selling "camouflage" or fake passports. Their makers tout them as "protection for security-conscious international travelers," but they are often sought by people wishing to conceal their identity, misrepresent themselves, or commit fraud.

Camouflage passports come from countries that no longer exist—Rhodesia, British Honduras, Zaire—or from made-up countries that never existed at all, like Freedonia. These often come with paperwork supporting your claim to be from this country. The people who sell them say they're useful if you're abducted or hijacked and you don't want your attackers to know your real citizenship. (If you're a citizen of Israel, the thinking goes, and you're abducted by Palestinians, it wouldn't hurt for them to think you're from Africa.)

I feel the same way about camouflage passports as I feel about identity theft: not a good move. Besides, where are you supposed to keep your real documents while you are being searched or robbed by hostiles? The companies that sell the camouflage passports forget to sell you luggage with hidden compartments. You also have to worry about speaking with the right accent and explaining why your passport has no stamps in it. Not to mention the fact that any customs agent who catches you with these papers will instantly think you're a criminal or, worse, a terrorist.

There's a fine, fine line between camouflage passports and fraud—a line that you will cross if you buy a fake passport with real stamps inside or try to use one to travel. Why risk it?

- **Guerrilla e-mail,** which is a disposable e-mail address that expires after an hour. Check out www.guerrillamail.com.
- **Digital mail,** an increasingly popular service offered by several companies. Have your snail mail forwarded to one of these places, and it will digitize all your mail, so you can log in and look at it online. Earth Class Mail (www.earthclassmail) is one such place. You can also use a company like Postful (www.postful.com) to send an e-mail that it will print out and send as a physical letter.
- **Freedom phones.** Available in Asia, these phones have all tracking devices removed. They are more expensive than common phone carriers, but are useful if you need to be in frequent communication. You can find them now at www .ptshamrock.com/auto/freedomphone.htm, but sources for these will change with time, so your best bet is to start with a Google search.

Remember that technology is constantly evolving and that hackers will always figure out a way to breach every "secure" new device. You're never going to be able to plunk down money for one state-of-the-art phone or computer and then enjoy worry-free security for the rest of your life. You're going to need to build layers of deception and fight off pursuers with constant vigilance. As you build your new life, these will truly be the most valuable tools in your tool kit.

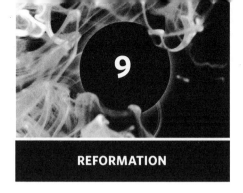

REFORMATION

I THREW A LOT AT YOU IN THE PREVIOUS CHAPTER. NOW IT'S TIME TO put those disappearing tools to use, whether you're planning to leave the country, avoid a stalker, or just fly a little lower under the radar.

Disappearing Day might be the most important day of your life. Think of it as your death and resurrection to a new life among the disappeared. (Just don't take that metaphor literally and fake your own death—it's not a great idea, as I'll explain in my chapter on "Pseudocide 101.")

You're about to join the ranks of people who live privately, quietly, and without fear. But once you make a run for it, there may be no turning back. So ask yourself: Is your exit plan flawless? Have you made yourself as difficult as possible to find? Have you double-checked your work by hiring a private investigator? Have you made even one tiny mistake?

If you're sure you've deleted or deviated all the information that exists about you, created false leads for an investigator to follow, and loaded up on your disappearing tools, you are ready to go. But keep this old saying in mind as you pack your bags:

 To be aware is to be alive.

Be vigilant as you leave. If you're skipping town, make sure you're not being watched, especially if you're the victim of a stalker. It wouldn't hurt to hire a private investigator to conduct surveillance on your pursuer to make sure he hasn't sent his goons to follow you or crawled onto the roof of your neighbor's house to watch your comings and goings.

ABANDONMENT

If you're leaving a husband, wife, or kids, I hope you're doing it the right way (if there is a right way) by finding a lawyer and giving them a chance to do the same. Do not go out for a newspaper and never return. That's just plain wrong.

If you can't afford a private investigator, use a good old-fashioned diversion. One of my clients was disappearing from an old business partner. On the day of his disappearance, a moving truck showed up, packed all of his belongings, and drove about an hour and a half . . . to a Goodwill store. The movers unloaded and then donated everything. My client knew his partner would be watching the house, so the surveillance team followed the truck to a dead-end while he hopped a train to better places.

No matter where you're headed, be it across town or out of the country, don't go straight there. Get on a plane to Toronto and fly to Puerto Rico and then hop on a puddle jumper if your final destination is St. Maarten. Get on a Greyhound to Raleigh and fly to Dallas to catch a plane to Salt Lake City. Do not underestimate the individual who is chasing you, and remember the Fluke Factor. Even something as minor as a magazine purchase in the airport could be your downfall.

In the airport, stay out of the newsstands and the bars and restaurants. Nobody needs to know you're making a trip except the people who wave you through the metal detector. Get through security, go straight to your gate, and wait.

I hope you have a pleasant trip. It will be even more pleasant if you've done the complicated yet crucial chores that are necessary for moving offshore: You have to set up your new home, figure out what you're going to do for money, think about how to communicate with your loved ones, and iron out the other details of day-to-day-living, such as where your kids are going to school, if they're coming along for the ride. As you do all this, you'll have one overarching goal:

 Become an entity with no traceable connections to people, places, or things.

You can easily accomplish this if you tackle your new life methodically and with care. Let's go over each item on your to-do list in order. Please note one thing before we start: This chapter deals with very general principles for relocating and rebuilding a new life, and succeeding chapters will address the specific details you're going to need to know if you're leaving the country, fleeing a stalker, or evading identity thieves. Turn to those chapters for more detail, and assume all of my advice about relocating in this chapter deals with domestic relocations.

With that said—let's look at the building blocks of your new life!

LIVING

The first thing you're going to want to take care of is your living situation. As you search for a new place to live, it is important to make sure that no real estate agent or leasing company runs your credit report. A skip tracer can easily extract the inquiry and figure out the name of the company that ran it. That's why we spent so much time getting Realtors to run credit reports when we were performing disinformation—it's a great way to divert pursuers running after you. The best way to avoid having a credit report run on you is to avoid Realtors and leasing companies altogether. I recommend you find an apartment on Craigslist or a community bulletin board that posts apartments for rent. These deals are more likely to be informal and not brokered by big real estate companies. Find a sublet if you can: It's ideal because the apartment information stays in the name of the landlord or the renter you're subletting from, not you. If you cannot locate a sublet, search for private rentals—that is, people renting out floors of their two- or three-family home.

If you can't find a sublet, I hope you were able to start a corporation before you left town. If not, do so now. Explain to real estate agents and others who rent out places that you are relocating to the area. Say your company will be paying your expenses and that you are interested in doing a corporate lease—meaning the lease is in the name of your corporation, not your name. Corporate leases are the best way to make sure that your name is not tied to the place where you live.

Open your utilities and cable in the name of your corporation, too, or better yet, find a living situation in which the landlord handles all of them.

COMMUNICATION

Now we're going to tackle your means of communication with the outside world. If you are not a stalking or abuse victim, I strongly suggest that you do not buy a home phone. If your life is in danger, however, go ahead and buy one. Just get it under the name of your corporation.

You can also get Internet service via the phone company, but never e-mail family and friends or bridge a connection from your old life to your new life.

You might be thinking: Never? How am I going to check in on my best friend when she's sick? Wish my little niece a happy birthday? Follow the latest news in my hometown? The short answer is: You're not. Communication between you and your loved ones is possible, but to stay safe, you're going to have to do this:

 Keep it short, keep it unpredictable, and keep it infrequent.

You'll have to do it using prepaid phones and public Internet connections and private mail drops and all the layers of anonymity and security I went over in the previous chapter.

It's tough. It's isolating. And most of the time, it sucks. We're touching on one of the most difficult aspects of disappearing:

 Disappearing is a tough thing to undergo psychologically.

You might feel despair when you realize that you can no longer just pick up the phone and call your family. You'll lose touch with a lot of people you care about. You're going to get lonely. Loneliness is a consequence of disappearing. You'll just have to decide whether it's an acceptable price to pay for the privacy you desire, or need.

While it *is* possible to communicate after disappearing, safe communications require careful preparation. My client Denise, a victim of an abusive ex-husband, communicated with her family using prepaid phones that she changed every couple of months and via a secret code she posted for them on free online classified pages. When she got a new prepaid cell phone, she'd post a specific car for sale: a Dodge. She'd write something like: "'98 Dodge with 95550 miles. Only 2 owners. Please call between 2 and 7 p.m.," and she would be remiss in placing a contact number for the ad. When her family saw that ad, they'd know her new contact number was (989) 555-0227.

She couldn't keep any one phone number for long, nor could she share her secret code with many of her friends, for fear they might tell her ex. But she had that lifeline.

BANKING

Your next task is getting your new bank accounts in order. Safe banking is a challenge, because banks are an easy place for an unscrupulous skip tracer to pretext for your personal information.

The next time you go into a bank, look around and you will see small signs that read, WE USE . . . . These signs describe a check service that banks use to investigate you before opening up an account. The service searches whether you've ever had overdrafts on past checking accounts or had an account closed because of overdrafts. And it can identify where you've applied for bank accounts.

Back in the Wild West days of my skip tracing, I became quite friendly with the tellers in my bank. I would stop by with doughnuts, coffee, chocolates, and other gifts that made them love to see me walk in the door. One day the branch manager was not at her desk, and I was at the window with the teller who managed the floor when the branch manager wasn't around.

I cashed a check and slid a $50 bill to the teller. "This is yours if you give me the password to the check service," I said.

She smiled and took the fifty. I cannot begin to tell you how many people I located, and how many bank accounts I pierced, with one toll-free number and six digits.

As long as banks use services like this—and hire people who are susceptible to bribes—your money trail is going to be easy to uncover. The *only* way you can spend securely is through a prepaid credit card.

MONEY AND EMPLOYMENT

There's no way around it: Disappearing without a trace takes money. How much depends on what you need to take with you when you go: the amount of furniture you have, the amount of money in your bank accounts, that kind of thing.

Most people who pick up and move are going to need to work to support themselves in their new location, since we aren't all lucky enough to be heiresses or lottery winners. Making money securely can be just as tricky as spending it securely. You can never be 100 percent sure that you're safe as long as you're paying income taxes. I know quite a few investigators who pretext Social Security, run a subject's number, and obtain a history of their tax contributions. No matter where you're working, if your employers made you sign an IRS form when you were hired, you're vulnerable to pretext. (If you work abroad for a company that doesn't pay U.S. taxes, you're a little safer, as a skip tracer will have to figure out your ID number in the foreign country to pretext its tax authority.)

My client Caroline was the victim of a very aggressive stalker, and she had to relocate. Caroline was a waitress by trade and found employment working off the books. When she filed her taxes, she

---

DISAPPEARING ON A BUDGET

A lot of you reading this book will feel overwhelmed by the cost of disappearing. Mail drops, prepaid phones, calling cards, plane tickets, private investigators, disinformation trips to random cities—all of these cost money. The cost of disinformation and reformation can easily climb into the thousands.

If you don't have a lot of money but have the time to save some up, I recommend you take that route. The more time and money you can invest in a thorough disappearance, the more confident you'll be once you're living under the radar.

However, if you have to disappear *now* and have nothing in your bank account, don't despair. Keep in mind that misinformation costs little to nothing, since all you're doing is calling up banks and Web sites and customer service departments to change your information. If you can't afford to do this with a prepaid phone, you can do it with a roll of quarters and a pay phone—or any public phone you can get your hands on.

Disinformation and reformation will be a little more difficult, but again, you're not entirely without options. Look for people who will help you out for little or nothing. If you are a stalking victim, this is easy: Your police department and local women's shelters are not going to charge for their services, and local self-defense instructors, coworkers, friends, and family will probably all be eager to chip in.

---

claimed what she made, but she provided her sister's address as her mailing address. Uncle Sam didn't suffer, and Caroline stayed safe.

Another client did computer consulting and could not work off the books, so his brother set up a company that allowed him to

If you need to skip town, find a sublet somewhere, since there'll be no required deposit and no credit report check. Flexible on your location? Look for a reasonable off-season vacation rental, such as a place on Myrtle Beach in the winter. I've seen hotel rooms there going for as little as $18/night when no tourists are around. You could also check out college dorms in the summer. Sometimes colleges will have available dorm rooms year-round—you might be able to go a whole year skipping from college to college.

If all else fails, see what your options are for free accommodation. One very cool travel trend that's cropped up in recent years is the proliferation of Web sites like www.couchsurfing.org and www.hospitalityclub.org, on which people volunteer their couches and spare bedrooms free of charge to travelers from all over the world.

Of course, you'll have to exercise extreme caution if you choose to spend the night at a stranger's house. But the great thing about these Web sites is that members come with references from the hundreds of thousands of other members on the site. You'll have a chance to do due diligence on the people you're thinking of visiting.

A few friends of mine have stayed at strangers' houses using these Web sites, and while they didn't always get along with their hosts, they never felt as if they were in danger. I think they're worth a look.

work under its name. At the end of each year, my client filed his taxes and his brother dissolved the corporation, paying and filing its taxes. Then the brother set up a new corporation in a different state. Business as usual began anew, and no one could skip-trace the corporation's tax records.

DEALING WITH DEBT

Wherever you're going, you do not want to leave bad credit behind. Do the best you can to pay what needs to be paid. Remember, FICO is a four-letter word. That credit score can really catch up with you in time and make life miserable if not handled properly.

Some of my clients who want to disappear want to trash their credit, not pay off their electricity, and leave the bills unattended. Big mistake. Look where you were five years ago: You probably did not anticipate disappearing today. You do not know what your situation will be like in the future.

Life is a rolling ball: Your stalker could end up in jail; you could make amends with your aggrieved business partner; your abusive ex could die. You might want to undisappear at some point, but you won't have that option if you leave debt behind.

Some clients have wanted to disappear because of debt. I always suggest that they deal with it properly by filing bankruptcy or arranging a payment plan with creditors.

Do not toss your bills into the wind. Remember, some skip tracer might find you in your new life and make your life miserable. It's complicated and scary to be in debt, but things will only get more complicated and scary when you're on the lam.

Remember this Ralph Waldo Emerson quotation: "A man in debt is so far a slave."

DRIVING

Any pursuer with half a brain will regularly check your motor vehicle record. You can't be Joe the bus driver in Albany and become Joe the bus driver in Oshkosh, because you'll have to transfer your driver's license. Nor can you safely switch your driver's license to your new location, even though most states require that you do. Nor can you ever get pulled over by a cop. So what do you do?

First, drive safely. Always check your lights and tires before you drive, don't make illegal turns, and obey the speed limit so that a cop never needs to pull you over. Second, drive with evidence that helps you explain why you can't transfer your driver's license to your new state.

My client Delia, who was a victim of her abusive ex-husband, moved to a different state and had to decide what to do about her car and driver's license. She owned her car outright, so we opened up a corporation and sold her car to it. She decided to keep her driver's license from her original state. This was in violation of state law, so in case she ever got pulled over, she kept a folder in her car with pictures of her face after she was beaten, hospital records to that effect, court documents, and a printout of her ex-husband's police record. That way, if she got pulled over, she could explain her situation. Cops have a good sense of when someone is lying and when that person is telling the truth.

If Delia was speeding or driving drunk, however, the cop might be justified in giving her a ticket, which would show up on her license. That ticket would give investigators a solid lead to her whereabouts. Therefore, Delia had to take extreme caution in her driving habits. It was a lifestyle change.

YOUR KIDS

Delia also had a small child who was just entering first grade. I located an excellent social worker in the area and explained Delia's situation. After looking deep into her case, the social worker was convinced she needed protection, so she arranged to enroll the child in school with a "clerical error" in the spelling of her name. That way, if a PI was searching through school records, there would be no hit. In time, Delia will correct the misspelling.

If you have children, their school records are a *huge* liability. Many, many people have been located by investigators and authorities when they ordered their children's school records transferred to a new district or signed their children up at a new school. If you are in danger, find a decent social worker or school employee who's willing to help you. Otherwise, look into alternative options, such as private or parochial school or homeschooling.

YOUR BACKUP PLAN

You know that old saying about the best laid plans of mice and men? Despite all your best efforts, you may be tracked to your new location. A stalker or an investigator might find you, or by some hideous coincidence, you might run into an old friend or a relative or even the person who's looking for you on the street. (I've heard of this happening.) Think through what you're going to do if that occurs.

If you're a victim, find a team of local allies who will spring to your aid. Look up women's shelters in the area, befriend a police detective, and get to know some social workers. If you're not a victim, take charge of planning your escape. Where are you going to go? What are you going to take with you? Where are you going to meet your spouse and children? How long will it take to perform misinformation and disinformation before you run off to a new location? Do you have enough money to disappear again? If not, start an emergency savings account today.

Suze Orman, the financial guru, tells everyone to pile up enough money to cover all your expenses for eight months if you lose your source of income. People who need to disappear should do that *and* add in the costs of what it will take to fly to a new location and rent a new place to live.

My client Delia made a very thorough backup plan for herself and her daughter. Her situation was very mobile, and most of her important belongings were in storage. She could be on the road immediately if her cover was blown. She and her daughter worked out a system of hand signals, code words, and signs to indicate to each other when something was wrong. They discussed how to get help and where to meet if one of them gave the sign.

I also taught Delia to create a "safe spot"—a place where she could rendezvous with her daughter, mother, and sister if she had to get out of town quickly. They picked a hotel room several towns away and worked out a plan in which the mother and sister would call her from a coin phone with arrangements for a new apartment.

EVERY CLIENT'S REFORMATION STORY IS DIFFERENT. THE NEXT several chapters deal with specific types of reformation—including disappearing from identity thieves, from a date, from a stalker, and from the country. But even within those categories, there's a great deal of variation about what you'll need to do to stay safe in your own particular circumstances. To start you thinking about what you'll need to do, here's one of my favorite client's stories.

CHARLIE

My client Charlie was a real estate investor who was involved with several partners buying and selling properties throughout Southern California. Charlie had the great American dream of doing that big deal that would put him on top of the world.

Unfortunately for Charlie, it did not work out that way. He put together a large deal in which he and several investors would buy an apartment complex in the South and hold it for a short time before flipping it to another buyer.

The deal went bad, and Charlie and the investors lost big. Then Charlie realized he had been more interested in getting the deal done than in doing due diligence on his fellow investors, which was a big mistake. One in particular was just not willing to accept that real estate can be a risky investment. Not long after the crumble, he sent two men to talk to Charlie on his behalf.

The conversation between Charlie and the two men—the two *scary* men, that is—went something like this: "We're here on behalf of Mr. X. You owe him X amount of dollars, and you will pay him back." The two men were quite convincing, and Charlie knew that his kneecaps and ribs were in danger.

Charlie needed time to pay off his disgruntled and dangerous investment partner. My suggestion to Charlie was that he open a corporation and live under the radar until he could pay his debt.

Charlie obtained a Main Drop, Bluff Box, Safe Box, and Burn Box a few towns away from where he lived and began to assemble his disappearing tools. He sent his prepaid phones, prepaid credit cards, and information about his other boxes to his Main Drop. He never brought any of that information into his house or office, because he knew his predators might break in and find it there.

Once Charlie opened his boxes, it was time for him to find a corporation he could exist under. He searched online, not from home or an Internet cafe, but from the streets. He went to a bookstore in another town and made handwritten notes from a few business books. He decided he wanted to open a corporation in Wyoming. He contacted a company that did incorporations, and it e-mailed him all of the papers he needed to fill out.

Charlie used a generic name for his corporation, like AAA Acme or something. He gave the state of Wyoming his Main Drop and a JConnect virtual phone number as his contact information. He paid for the corporation with a prepaid credit card.

Because of the ongoing demands of his business deals, Charlie had to be in contact with clients and associates. He couldn't stop making phone calls, nor could he disconnect his existing phone line, since it was in the Rolodexes of so many important contacts. So he purchased several prepaid cell phones, making sure to pick companies from smaller carriers without customer service departments, huge national databases, and 24/7 help lines.

We took Charlie's existing cell phone and used call forwarding to connect the number to a prepaid phone. Then we used call forwarding *again* to send that phone's calls to a second prepaid phone. A skip tracer who pretexted Charlie's main cell phone company might have been able to get the number the phone was forwarded to, and if he was successful at that, he might have been able to get a GPS location on the first prepaid phone. You can never be too safe. Charlie had a lot of phones to keep track of and topped off, but he could be reasonably certain that no one pretexting his old cell phone company could find his current contact number.

When he contacted clients, Charlie only used his prepaid cell phone. For added security, he used a spoof card, which changed the number that appeared on clients' caller IDs to one based in the United Kingdom. Any client who saw his caller ID or pressed *69 would believe Charlie was in the U.K.

Slowly, Charlie was able to earn back the money to pay his investor. He survived with his kneecaps intact.

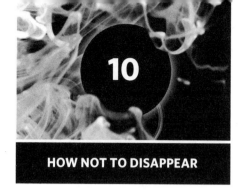

HOW NOT TO DISAPPEAR

I HOPE THAT THE PAST FEW CHAPTERS HAVE FILLED YOU WITH IDEAS about how to disappear safely, securely, and with panache. But maybe you feel like a section was missing from the "reformation" chapter. What about fake IDs, you ask? What if you think the safest thing for you to do is just ditch your old identity and buy a new one?

Wrong. If you think buying a fake identity is the way to go, this is the chapter you need to read. This chapter is about all the mistakes you can make on your way to a life among the disappeared, and stealing an identity is mistake No. 1. The other big mistake is trying to live a life that's more or less identical to the one you left behind.

Throwing out *everything* from your previous life—including your passport—and throwing out *nothing* are two extremes that you must avoid on your disappearing journey. Let me show you why this is the case.

I'M NOT SOME BOY SCOUT OR A HUGE DEFENDER OF JOHNNY LAW. I firmly believe that what you decide to do once you disappear is up to you. As long as you're not hurting anyone or infringing on other people's rights, what you do once you disappear is not my concern.

That said, let me tell you something:

 Assuming a false identity is a bad idea.

If you aren't a criminal or an international spy, you do not need a new identity to disappear safely and discreetly. Why commit fraud if you don't have to? It's a headache, and you're probably going to get caught, even if you read one of the many books and Web sites out there that explain how to do it.

In the past, identity theft was relatively easy. A popular yet morbid way to obtain a new identity was via a cemetery search: You would wander around a cemetery until you located a child who was born around the same year you were and who had died by the age of five. From there, you would obtain a birth certificate, a Social Security number, and other identifiers in the child's name, and presto, you'd have a brand spanking new identity.

You can't do that anymore. That method only worked in the pre-computer era. Today, automated systems exchange vital-statistic, Social Security, and motor vehicle data between government agencies, and the feds will know in an instant if you try to steal a dead person's ID. If you get busted, the charges will send you to the can for a long vacation.

Every day, I receive e-mails from individuals requesting my services to assist in obtaining new identities, passports, driver's licenses, visas, and birth certificates. I don't know where they got the idea that I dabble in that stuff. I assume that most of these inquiries are fakes from law enforcement, which is understandable—they're just doing their job. What is not understandable is why an individual would believe that I would offer such services—or even the hint that I performed them—over the Internet. Here's an important thing to remember:

 Avoid people who sell fake documents on the Web: They don't know what they're doing.

If these people were experts in international identity theft—the kind of people who could get you foolproof IDs in this day and age, with massive police crackdowns on ID operations all over the globe—do you really think they would advertise this on Google? *All* the people who peddle these services online are crooks and quacks. They might as well be selling secret decoder rings and love potion No. 9. Do not fall for their schemes.

DON'T ADMIT ILLEGAL BEHAVIOR IN AN E-MAIL

If you are planning on an exit and perhaps doing something illegal, whether it's stealing an identity or anything else, do NOT e-mail anyone asking for illegal information or services. You need to assume that everyone you contact is either law enforcement or will drop a dime on you to law enforcement.

During the height of my pretext days, I knew that I was participating in a legal gray area and that I could get into a lot of trouble doing what I did, so I ran it like a drug business. What does that mean? It means I was fucking paranoid, is what it means. I operated on the assumption that law enforcement was watching my every move and that every client had the potential of dropping a dime on me.

I am sure Pablo Escobar or Howard Marks never e-mailed a stranger for advice on their drug-smuggling businesses. If you are breaking the law and need to hoof it, make it a solo venture.

The people who *really* specialize in fake documents sell them face-to-face. But that doesn't mean you can trust any guy you stumble upon in a dark alley. (Yes, people do sell these documents in dark alleys. In the U.K., they recently busted an organization selling passports on the streets.) No matter who you buy from, you have no way of knowing whether you're getting a passport with a number that's still valid or a bar code that actually scans. What about the holograms? This is not like passing fake twenties to a bartender. This is the big time.

Buying an identity from a friend of a friend might seem like a safe bet, but it comes with its own set of risks. Do you really trust this person? You might hit the bank account with your new ID and deposit your life savings, only to receive a letter a few weeks later that the IRS has levied your account and your new balance is zero. Why? Because the moron whose identity you purchased owed several thousand dollars in back taxes. Ouch.

What if your new identity has a criminal record? What if it's for a terrorist on the no-fly list? Imagine showing up at the airport and not being able to go to your new home. I just don't think the risks are worth it.

Let's say that by some miracle, you manage to nab convincing and clean counterfeit papers. There are aspects of this crime that I bet you haven't considered: How are you going to test your papers to make sure they work? Do you book an international trip and just wing it at customs? Do you speed along in your car till you get pulled over and have a cop run your new license? Perhaps you'll walk into a Social Security office with your new birth certificate and apply for a Social Security number at the age of thirty-five, after explaining that you've been living in a cave since you were fifteen?

The only way you can test your new identity papers is to use them. You'll have to stroll into customs with that fake passport. If you do, you better be one cool cat and not get that *Midnight Express* look—heart racing, face sweating—that red-flags you to the back room. I've been in that room. It's a tough place to be. You'll want to avoid that experience.

Being the long-haired, goateed, shady-looking character I am, screening and questioning are just par for the course when I go to the airport. I must fit the drug-smuggler profile. A few years back, I was returning to the States from a trip to Ireland, and at the first entry point, the official typed in my passport information, and a funny look appeared on his face. He pointed to the other side of the room and said, "Take your stuff and go there." I walked over, thinking, *This is going to be fun.*

An official walked into the room and snapped on some rubber gloves. "Put your bag on the counter, unzip, and step back," he told me. I did.

He jumped back. "What is *that*?" he said. This was right around the time of the anthrax attacks.

"Baby powder," I said.

He began to ask me a litany of questions as he was inspecting my passport: "What were you doing in Ireland? Did you see any businesspeople? Did you go anywhere else than Ireland? Where did you stay? Who did you stay with?"

He bent over his computer and typed in my passport number. He got a puzzled look on his face like the first guy and called for another officer to look at the screen. Then they switched computers and decided to call in another official.

After a few minutes, a top brass official swished into the room. He took my passport and walked off while the other two rummaged through my clothes and battered me with even more questions. I was nervous. I had no clue what was going on. I tried to be calm, but in my head I was thinking, *If I act calm they will think I am hiding something.* So I decided I wouldn't act calm, but then I thought, *If I act afraid they will think I am hiding something.* My brain was shooting off a million messages at once, I was sweating bullets, and I had done nothing wrong. My heart was pounding.

The top brass official returned forty minutes later and headed right toward me with an unpleasant look on his face. The other two guys were observing him as well, probably waiting to pounce on the Frank M. Ahearn order.

The brass handed me my passport and apologized. It was a case of mistaken identity. I scooped up all of my belongings and rushed outside to the comfort of three shots of tequila.

I don't know why I was stopped. Maybe there's some IRA terrorist with my name. But I had no choice but to stay there until they said otherwise. Try that with a fake passport and see how well you stand up.

I am totally against new identities. Imagine you are now Mr. Vincent Vega from Palm Springs, and you're hanging out with your lady friend and her family sipping piña coladas, and over walks your best friend from high school. This numbnut starts calling you by your real name, Dexter Plaidpants. Try explaining that to the table. New identities are like roulette. It's only a matter of time until your number comes up!

DON'T SCRAP YOUR WHOLE ID WHEN YOU DISAPPEAR. WORK TO make your own legal records as invisible as possible, and distract your pursuers with a tangle of disinformation.

At the same time, however, make sure that you've left *some* of your old life behind. You should leave town with your real passport and birth certificate, but leave behind the hobbies, business contacts, and routines that characterized your old life. Why? Skip tracers will probably know about them, and they'll be searching for you with them in mind. As difficult as this is to accept, there's a harsh truth about disappearing:

 Disappearing is a lifestyle change. Change your passions, or they'll become your pitfalls.

Back when I was a skip tracer, I used people's hobbies to locate them all the time. I call one of my favorite stories about that "The Tale of the Artful Dodger."

THE ARTFUL DODGER

Once in a while, a client would ask if I could serve process on a subject, meaning serve a person who was being sued with legal papers. I was never a big fan of our court system, but over the years, some hard serves came my way, and I could never say no to a good challenge.

The Artful Dodger was one such challenge. He was an art dealer who had reneged on a $400,000 payment for an antique car he'd bid on at auction. The auction company filed suit, and I had to locate the Dodger to slap him with the papers.

My preliminary search revealed that he lived in a brownstone on Manhattan's Lower East Side. A wrought-iron gate protected his gallery/home. The gallery was not open to the public, but by appointment only, which presented a major problem. He refused to meet with most people who came into the gallery, and I couldn't just waltz right in and serve him.

All of this was happening a few weeks after Keith Haring, the acclaimed artist who climbed to fame via the New York City subway system, passed away. I contacted the Artful Dodger at home and introduced myself as Pat Brown, who was representing a family interested in selling a few pieces of Haring's artwork.

The Dodger said I should send him some Polaroids. I responded, "I only have one set. If you're not interested, can you point me toward someone who would be?" I knew that the prospect of snatching up the Harings would make most art dealers salivate.

He suggested I come to his gallery.

I made my way to the brownstone and rang the bell, only to be greeted by the Artful Dodger's boy toy. I stood between the wrought-iron gate and the front door, and he asked for the photos. "I am not leaving," I said. "It's my only set."

He assured me that he would show the Artful Dodger the photos and I could wait outside.

"No," I said. "You're wasting my time." I turned to exit, and out stepped an older white man whose face resembled the one I'd seen in the auction photo. My heart beat faster, but I kept up my façade. "Don't waste my fucking time. I am here to see . . ."

He stepped toward me and identified himself, inviting me into the gallery. I was holding an envelope full of what he must have assumed were the photos. Wrong! The door behind me began to close slowly, and I realized to my horror that it was one of those doors that required you to be buzzed in and out. *Oh shit!* I thought. This was going to have to end here.

"Are you [the Artful Dodger's real name]?" I asked one more time.

Again, he confirmed.

I thrust the envelope at him. "Well, you've been served," I said.

His face turned a deep flamingo pink: white for shock, red for anger. Feet, don't fail me now, I thought. I grabbed the door before it shut and flung myself out. He was right behind me, and it was possible steam was shooting out of his ears. Luckily, his front gate opened without fail.

On the sidewalk, I made a beeline down the block. The Artful Dodger was right behind, yelling and waving his hands in the air. I picked up the pace—that lasted for two seconds—and then, wheezing, I resorted to good old New York City–style dodging, tipping garbage cans to block his path. He started tossing lids at me like Frisbees.

Finally, the process papers winged past me, and I hung a right down Lexington Avenue. After weaving in and out of suits for a while, I ducked into a bar and ordered three shots of tequila, safe. I had lived through another day.

WHAT'S THE MORAL OF THIS STORY? THE ARTFUL DODGER MADE himself vulnerable because his attempt to "disappear" was only half-assed. He lived at an unlisted address and hid himself from strangers, but he couldn't help himself from continuing to collect art, which meant that with a little subterfuge, anyone who knew about that vocation could arrange a face-to-face meeting. If you're going to disappear, stop doing all the things that people would expect you to do. Don't collect. Don't indulge. And for the love of God:

Don't Google yourself once you've hit the road.

After Olivia Newton-John's ex-lover Patrick McDermott disappeared, the ingenious folks at *Dateline NBC* were able to catch him by setting up a Web site called "Find Patrick McDermott" and telling Patrick's family about it. Lo and behold, a few weeks later, the site got a cluster of visits from the vicinity of Acapulco, Mexico. That's where he was. His vanity was his undoing.

"Just be yourself" is the *opposite* of what you should do once you hit the road. I have as many anecdotes to prove it as you could possibly want to read: The bookworm who transferred his Barnes & Noble membership to his new house in the Dominican Republic, the foodie who couldn't say no to home delivery of his favorite meals. I found them all. Use your disappearance as an excuse to try something new!

11

DISAPPEAR FROM IDENTITY THIEVES

YOU MIGHT HAVE THUMBED THROUGH THE PREVIOUS CHAPTERS thinking, this isn't for me. I'm no criminal. I'm not trying to run away. I don't need to skip town or leave the country. No one's coming after me.

Well, I've got news for you: It wouldn't hurt you to disappear a little. Yes, you. Companies are still buying and selling and trading your information all the time, and the deals that got you on some annoying mailing list or telemarketing database yesterday might lead to identity theft and financial ruin tomorrow. Do you really want your contact information, credit score, age, and family connections splashed all over the Internet for everyone to see? How could that possibly be a good thing?

Think of this chapter as "disappearing lite" for those of you who just want to make yourselves a little less vulnerable to identity thieves—to reduce your information footprint, your digital footprint. To protect yourself from what we in the business call **intrusion,** you can take several preemptive steps to secure your personal information.

First, let me define "intrusion" for you.

> **Intrusion, n.:** a criminal act in which an individual claiming to be you uses your personal information for financial gain.

There are six types of intrusion:

Business intrusion occurs when a criminal uses your corporation or trade name for his own personal profit. People in the Mafia do this all the time. If a guy who owns a restaurant owes them money, they'll move in and demand access to his company line of credit. Then they'll max out his credit cards buying steaks or lobster and sell these on the black market, keeping the profit while poor Johnny Restaurant has to deal with the debt.

Criminal intrusion happens when a criminal is arrested and poses as you, so the criminal charges are filed in your name, with your contact information.

This is ludicrously easy to do. I recently read a story about how it happened to some kid named Armon in New Orleans. He lived with his parents, was quiet and shy, and didn't drive, and yet one day he got a letter saying he needed to show up in traffic court for driving without a license. A few weeks later, he got a letter saying he could avoid doing time for his misdemeanor marijuana conviction if he took some treatment courses. He was baffled.

Then he opened a newspaper and saw an article about another teenager doing time in the county jail. The guy in jail said his name was Armon _____: the same name as the innocent kid reading the newspaper. Armon's last name was complicated and ethnic, so there was no way this could be a coincidence. The teenager in jail was pretending to be him.

Turns out an old friend of Armon's had turned to a life of crime, and he was going around giving cops his friend's name. Even though he wasn't carrying ID, he had Armon's address memorized, and the cops were dumb enough to take him at his word. By the time poor innocent Armon discovered the mix-up, his ex-friend had left jail and nobody could find him. Armon had to file a court motion to clear his name. Otherwise, he would come up as a criminal on any future job search—just because some moron memorized his address.[3]

Financial intrusion, the form of intrusion we hear about most often, occurs when someone uses your wonderful personal credit to obtain credit cards, checks, loans, and other instruments of gain. Hardly a day goes by when we don't hear about that happening. Chances are good that some form of financial intrusion will happen to you at some point, whether it's someone stealing your credit card information to go crazy buying lotto tickets at a gas station or something much worse, like someone opening up and maxing out a $30,000 AmEx in your name.

Many people refer to financial intrusion as "identity theft," but we in the business use that term more strictly as a synonym for **identity intrusion** or **"ghosting."** This is the act of assuming someone else's whole identity to live as that person, involving things like fake passports and birth certificates. Someone who has committed identity intrusion represents himself as someone else not just on paper to financial institutions, but to almost everyone he knows, almost every day of his life. This is classic con-man stuff.

Synthetic intrusion or **"synthetic identity theft"** is a scary new variety of identity intrusion in which a criminal uses bits and pieces of your information. For example, he'll combine your real Social Security number with a different name and date of birth. The result is that two identities are created under one identifier, and with them two credit reports, two criminal backgrounds, two motor vehicle histories, etc. Synthetic intrusion is very difficult to track because the intruder will have a separate credit profile, and it might be months or

---

3 Winkler-Schmit, David. (2009, March 23). Mistaken Identity at Orleans Parish Prison. The Gambit. Retrieved from http://bestofneworleans.com/gyrobase/Content?oid=oid:52763, 11 April 2010.

years before you realize that someone else is tarnishing the reputation associated with your Social.

If you become a victim of synthetic intrusion, my suggestion is to contact a good private investigator and hire him or her to track down the thief or at least gather more information about him. May I recommend the services of Eileen Horan, my business partner? Otherwise, try to get one recommended by a family member or business associate.

Medical intrusion happens frequently in our society, sometimes with the consent of the person whose identity is being stolen. This is when a person uses another's identity to obtain medical care. If two twin sisters live together and one is employed and the other isn't, the unemployed one might pose as the other to visit the doctor when she gets strep throat.

I have to be honest—I can understand this one, given the state of our health care system. But if someone does this for expensive medical treatments without your knowledge, you can pay a pretty penny in premiums. Not to mention the fact that you may face lifetime difficulty obtaining insurance coverage due to your "preexisting condition."

These forms of intrusion are all relatively simple to commit—except for maybe identity intrusion, which requires the money and determination to get the proper paperwork and build a new life as someone else. Criminals can easily get your information from a number of sources: the mail, the trash, a retail location where your card is double-swiped, the back-end offices of credit card companies.

Can you prevent intrusion? Ultimately, I don't think you can. But you can make it difficult for criminals by using a few disappearing techniques. Here's what you should do.

Fight deception with deception.

It wouldn't hurt you to do a little misinformation on your records. Call up your utility companies, tell them you've misspelled your name, and "correct" it so your details don't come up when a thief pretexts the company in search of your information. When you're opening a new account with a customer service rep—be it the phone company, the video store, or the local library—try to decline giving any information at all. Ask them why they need to know.

FRANK'S PHILOSOPHY

It really irritates me when I call the cell, cable, or credit card company and it wants to update my information. You can't even go to a retail store these days without being asked for your e-mail address or phone number. Do they really need my number? The answer is no. It seems like Big Business is more concerned with gathering your information than with providing the services they advertise.

If you can't get out of giving them your information, change it a little bit. If you were born in August 1972, tell them your birth date is September 1969. When the rep asks where you work, give the phone number of the local prosecutor's office. When they ask for a home or work or cell phone number, give them numbers for Chinese, pizza, and falafel delivery (at least they'll know where to turn for great fast food in your area).

Consider inverting the last few digits of your Social Security number for personal security reasons. This is not exactly legal, but you're not hurting anyone by doing it, and that way you can be sure that thieves will never extract correct information on you.

Many companies offer password protections on accounts these days. People ask me all the time whether these make any difference. The truth is: sometimes they do, sometimes they don't, but it's better to have a password on your account than not. It's one more barrier between the thief and your information.

 Passwords are a plus.

Whatever password you create, make sure that it's a secure one and that you avoid the following common password mistakes: using children's names, pets' names, birthdays, the word "password," your hobby, your mother's maiden name, your favorite sports team—or recycling the same password you use for every other log-in, from Facebook to e-mail to your checking account.

Several companies pimp out identity theft programs, but I have yet to see any that would actually stop the theft from happening. They are mostly response-related services—it's not as if someone can zap a crook with lightning the instant he tries to use your credit card.

Worse yet, these services cost money. They charge you a monthly fee to monitor your credit report, which in my opinion is something credit card companies should be doing for free. But I have to admit that these services are inexpensive and can alert you to intrusion before the crime becomes devastating. You might want to consider signing up for one.

Keep in mind that no service or program will ever protect you as well as you can with a little vigilance and common sense.

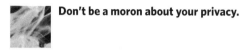 **Don't be a moron about your privacy.**

I have been in airports where I overheard people speaking with their credit card companies. Right there in the middle of the gate, they yelled out their name, Social, and account number. Anybody listening could have taken down their information and used their card while the fool was in the air. Be careful where you make calls for banking. Do not call your credit card or bank from public places unless it's imperative—and in that case, hit the bathroom and whisper from a stall.

Look around you when you're about to use your credit card or hit the ATM. Crooks often lurk in public places with cameras, taking pictures of people flashing their credit cards and entering in their PIN (personal identification number). If your credit card number is visible on the photo, say *sayonara* to your cash.

Pay attention to what customer service representatives ask you to divulge. Sometimes, employees in the back offices of these companies make a grab for your information after they handle your transactions. If you speak to an employee and feel that he or she is taking more information than necessary or asking for more than he or she needs to know, request to speak to a supervisor and relate the conversation to that supervisor.

Don't use your credit card in a retail store where you can't make the swipe yourself. Otherwise, you can never be sure whether cashiers are double-swiping: that is, swiping your card through the machine for the real transaction, then using a hidden device to swipe your card again and extract your information. If you're in one of the few remaining mom-and-pop stores that don't have a self-swipe machine, pay in cash.

Restaurants and bars are also risky. Waiters and bartenders usually take your card away and swipe it, leaving you vulnerable to a secondary fraudulent swipe . . . or a guy with a pen and paper who copies down your number, expiration date, and security code. Pay for your meals in cash.

Not a fan of toting cash everywhere? Make like my celebrity clients:

 Use prepaid credit cards.

Yes, prepaid credit cards. You might not draw gasps of admiration when you whip out your Achieve Card or All Access, but unlike your friends who tote American Express, you can go to sleep at night knowing your credit is safe.

Don't be embarrassed. All my celebrity clients use prepaid cards. They get one sent to their private mail drop and have their assistant keep it topped up at local convenience stores. No fuss, no fraud.

A private mail drop? Yes, it's what celebrities do to keep their mail private, and you should consider it, too. It's ridiculously easy for thieves to steal your information from the mail. If you live in a house, there is a good chance that your mail is put in an unlocked box curbside or by your front door. A thief could simply walk up to the box and grab some bills. If he's smart, he'll return the following day to put them back, having opened, copied, and resealed everything. You will never know until it's too late.

Even if you do have a lock on your mailbox, it's easy to pop those little locks. (Not that I speak from experience . . . or do I?) Therefore:

 Your best bet for secure mail is always going to be an unbreakable, unpretextable, indoor private mail drop.

Even if someone manages to steal your key, there's a constant flow of people at these locations. There are also plenty of cameras watching at all times. You can nail whoever tries to steal from you.

If you refuse to listen to me, fine—but please, please: Never leave your outbound mail in your curbside mailbox. If you're leaving checks, bill payments, and tax forms in there, you're just asking to have your identity stolen. Why are you even reading this book if you care so little? .

Can't afford a private mail drop?

 Go paperless with your bills.

Pay all of them online. (I'm assuming your utility companies have secure sites.) If you choose to do paperless billing and payment, the first thing you should do after you sign up is enroll yourself for text message alerts, so you get a text message to your cell phone every time someone makes a purchase with your credit card. You'll know instantly if someone steals something on your card—and on the flip side, you'll know that someone's hacked your account if you make a purchase and *don't* get a text.

Signing up for text alerts is only a good idea if you're an average person who's not being pursued by a skip tracer, a stalker, or Johnny Law. If someone pursuing you manages to get hold of your text history, he'll be able to surmise your location based on where you're making charges.

When you sign up for online billing, do not use the same e-mail address that you use for contacting work, friends, and family. Create a separate e-mail address that you use for bill payments only. Make sure this e-mail doesn't include your first or last name or any other obvious identifying details.

If you're not especially concerned that someone is looking for your personal information, it's OK to use just one e-mail for all of your online bills—but change the password frequently, using a mix of numbers and letters.

Memorize all of your passwords. Write them down on paper and keep them stored in a secure place, like a safe. *Don't* keep them saved on your hard drive. Computers are just too easy to hack—treat them with respect and a healthy dose of fear.

THAT BRINGS ME TO MY NEXT TOPIC: COMPUTERS. I'M NOT A BIG computer lover. Have you ever watched that show *Battlestar Galactica*? The premise is that crazy hacker robots have all but annihilated humanity. They've attacked our cities and our military, and only one warship has survived because its grizzled old captain didn't trust technology and refused to link his computers to the military mainframe. Because the captain refused to participate in the whole technological shitshow, he survived the robot hacker apocalypse. I try to be like that captain. So should you.

Computers become obsolete almost as soon as you buy them, so I imagine you're going through a new one every couple of years.

When you throw one out, don't just put it on the curb or give it to charity after chucking all your files into the Windows "recycling bin." Thieves go through trash cans and charity bins all the time to locate information from discarded computers—and most of us make their job easy. I have even seen people put their laptops out on the sidewalk (or Craigslist, or Freecycle) with a sign that says, WORKS. These people are insane, or stupid, or both.

You can buy software that supposedly wipes your hard drive clean, but who really knows if everything is deleted? I don't. That's why I do things my own way.

THE FRANK M. AHEARN GUIDE TO
DESTROYING A COMPUTER

1. Get a hammer and whack the hard drive a few times.
2. Put the hard drive in a bucket and fill it with Lysol or turpentine. Please do so in a well-ventilated area so you don't get sick and sue me. Keep out of reach of children and pets.
3. Let the hard drive sit for a few days, rinse it off, wrap it in plastic, and then put it in the freezer for a few more days.
4. Take your hard drive out of the freezer, drive it to the nearest ocean or large body of water, and toss it in. Yes, it's littering. Go plant a tree, and you'll feel better.

You should treat old cell phones with similar distrust. Whether you're throwing your phone in the trash or giving it away to a friend, delete your phone book and restore the phone to factory settings. You'd be surprised how much I've managed to extract from cell phones over the course of my career: not just contact information, but also e-mail addresses, passwords, text messages, and calling history.

Does your phone have a word-recognition or T9Word program installed on it? Pretty cool how it keeps learning new words and phrases, right? Well, if I find your old cell phone and discover that your most-used T9 words are "Guadalajara," "bank account," "contraband," and "millions," then you're in trouble.

I am pretty clumsy and tend to drop my cell phones and break them. I have a drawer filled with broken ones. When I get around to it, I wrap them in a bag, go caveman on them with a sledgehammer, then drop them down a sewer. Sure, it's not technical, but it's the best way I know to keep prying eyes away from my calling history.

My general principle is this:

 When you're done with it, destroy.

That applies to paperwork as well as electronic devices. If you receive any bills, draft contracts, or other sensitive information in the mail, get a paper shredder and get rid of them when you're done. Don't go for some bottom-of-the-line $13 piece of crap shredder—get a good one that cross-shreds in multiple directions, so your papers are impossible to put back together.

Don't put all your shredding in one bag when you toss it. Put it in several bags so a thief couldn't possibly have all the pieces of the puzzle. Mix it with the most disgusting trash you have: sauerkraut, mashed potatoes, baby's diapers. Better yet: flush your shredding. Even better: burn it. Back when I had a yard, I'd toss my shredding in a metal can and light a match. If you choose this route, keep a fire extinguisher nearby. Safety first, folks.

It's up to you how you destroy your sensitive material, but it's imperative that you destroy it. Always use common sense and err on the side of caution if you're not sure whether a criminal would be interested in a particular piece of information. If you want to avoid being one of the millions of people whose information is bought, sold, hijacked, and abused every year, you have to stay one step ahead of the people who want to take it from you. And that includes Big Brother.

DISAPPEAR IN SOCIAL MEDIA

IF YOU'RE DEAD SET ON SOCIAL NETWORKING OR CONTRIBUTING TO the blogosphere, I wish you luck. I think it's a terrible idea. I'd never want other people to know that much of my business.

But I recognize that I'm a little . . . paranoid. Plenty of people just can't stay away from Facebook and Twitter and Blogspot, and some of you will need to be on sites like these because your livelihoods hang in the balance. Maybe you're a marketing professional or the editor of a newsletter or the organizer of a group, and you need to be able to reach out to customers or readers or your audience. Maybe you want to monitor sites like Facebook to see whether there's any chatter about you. Maybe you live your life out in the open and are not worried about anyone knowing where you live or who your friends are . . . but you still want to make sure you're not opening yourself up to any unnecessary vulnerabilities.

Being the positive individual that I am, I will look on the bright side of social networking and show you how to use it as safely as possible. As Facebook says, "It's complicated"—but it's doable.

I learned how to disappear on social networks because I was paid to. I had written it off as an impossibility because I'd located targets based on their Internet activity more times than I could count. There was the time a woman who suspected her husband was cheating on her gave us a list of his favorite nicknames, and inside of an hour,

FRANK'S RULES FOR THE WEB

1. Every time you want to construct a Web page or sign up for a social media site, make a new, anonymous e-mail address for that specific purpose.

2. When you're picking an e-mail address or a Web URL, get one that ends with a foreign extension like .co.uk or .de. People will assume that's where you live.

3. If you need to include any other contact information on that site, such as a phone number or address, make sure it's for a JConnect number or a mail drop located very far from you.

4. Never use your real name on the Internet. Use a misspelling, or better yet, a pseudonym.

5. Anything you do online that costs money should be paid for with a pre-paid credit card.

6. Never trust anyone you meet or anything you see on Facebook. Use it and its competitors as entertainment—nothing more.

7. Don't use Facebook to communicate with your friends, and don't use it to find long-lost loved ones. Use the telephone, write people letters, and meet them in person. If you want to find contact information for an old friend, use an online phone book—or hire a private investigator. Don't trust what you see online.

8. Don't use networking sites to cheat on your spouse or commit a crime!

we found him under one of them on a dating Web site. Then there were all the times I'd pretexted subjects' friends and family members using numbers I found on Facebook. I still have the script in my head: "Hi, this is Pat Brown from UPS, and we have a water-damaged package waiting here for you. Looks like the return address is someone named—Stefan? Stefano? Stephen? [Or some other mispronunciation of the subject's name.] When are you available to sign for it at your home? Three p.m.? Thank you, and one other thing—we have to send a damaged-package notice to you and the person who sent this, but there doesn't seem to be an address here for him. Can you help us with that?" Most people like being helpful.

Yes, I was pretty skeptical about a person's chances of staying private in social media. But then an e-mail showed up in my inbox from a person who was interested in creating a religious newsletter. This guy was a bright, successful businessman who didn't want his spiritual and working lives to collide, and he needed help creating an online community that was not in any way attached or connected to his name. He wanted to promote that community on Facebook and MySpace, but he couldn't do so personally.

His religion wasn't my flavor of choice, but hey, I don't judge. He wasn't spewing hate, and I'm all about the First Amendment. So I accepted the case.

My client's first task was to create several e-mail addresses from free sites all over the world. He used an Internet cafe, but over the years, I have come to believe that a laptop connected to free, public wireless Internet is safer than any cafe. You never know who's watching you on an in-store camera or whether someone has installed tracking software on the unit you're using. So if you really need your activity to stay anonymous, it's best to use public wireless.

Next, my client and I bought some prepaid credit cards for all of the expenses that would be associated with this venture: a printer, a distributor for his newsletter, phone line, fax number, mailbox, and Web hosting. This guy wanted to be able to chat with people on the phone and to receive and send letters, but he didn't want them to have any clue where he lived. Fortunately, thanks to JConnect and private mailing companies, that was no problem.

We located and bought several mail drops in the Caribbean, all of them in different countries. One mail drop served as his primary mailbox, and we paid the providers of the other two to forward whatever they got to his primary box. We set up a toll-free JConnect phone and fax line, using a different e-mail address and prepaid credit card for each. And then we bought a site name through a popular Web hosting service, opting for a URL that ended in .de. The JConnect numbers we bought, and the e-mail address he designated as his official contact for the newsletter, looked German as well: It's every bit as easy to buy a German phone number or e-mail address from the United States as it is to buy an American one.

We sent the German e-mail and phone number to a printer in Tennessee, who was more than happy to print this religious newsletter for a Mr. and Mrs. Hans and Gretchen Lugner of Germany. Then we found small distribution companies all over the United States that were willing to spread the good word of Jesus on behalf of the "Lugners." We were almost ready to start printing.

But first, it was up to the Frank Ahearn Marketing Team to build some buzz about the newsletter. I went to Fifth Avenue, picked up some free wireless on my laptop, and created about a dozen fake e-mails. Within an hour, I had created pages for about fifteen different Jesus freaks on Facebook and MySpace, and wouldn't you know—they all loved my client's newsletter. These "people" also posted about the newsletter on various religious blogs and message boards. Suddenly, my client had a following.

I set up a Facebook page for Hans and Gretchen Lugner and made a fan page for the newsletter, on which all of its loyal readers (i.e., Frank, Frank, and Frank) posted adoring comments. Then—yet another reason I'm probably going to hell—I found a bunch of photos from some random family's Web site, hit right click, saved them all, and posted them on the page. Hey, that's what happens when you put your photos online. People like me steal them.

Real people (or at least they looked like real people) eventually found my links and comments. They commented on Hans and Gretchen's Facebook page and nice family photos, and from there they followed my link to the newsletter. I used a search-engine optimization program, Trellian SubmitWolf, to make the newsletter as Googleable as possible, and within just a few months, my client had a thriving Web site that was totally disconnected from his name or private information.

I will grudgingly admit that it *is* possible to do what my client did: establish an online presence and conduct business in social media without endangering yourself too much. But you have to be very careful.

13

DISAPPEAR FROM A FROG

LET'S FACE IT: DATING IS NOT ALWAYS FUN. DO THEY STILL SELL THOSE cheesy key chains that say, "You have to kiss a lot of frogs in order to meet your prince?" Well, thanks to the Internet, you can now kiss six or seven frogs at the same time for the low, low cost of $30 a month.

I say no thanks. But if you choose to say yes to the ever-expanding world of Internet dating, you can use misinformation and some basic skip-tracing techniques to make sure you don't end up with a stalker in your driveway. I'm going to address these tips to the ladies, but they absolutely apply when the roles are reversed.

The best way to save yourself from the frogs is preparation, preparation, preparation. When you fill out your online profile, put up only one picture—remember, photos can be copied and manipulated. Do not put down your real zip code; use one from a few towns over. No one needs to know your exact location.

When all the frogs are e-mailing you and you're ready to respond:

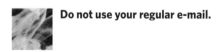 **Do not use your regular e-mail.**

Make a Yahoo! or Hushmail account and don't put down any identifiers, such as your real name or address. Use one e-mail address for each frog on your list. This way, if you want to stop communicating with someone, you can just delete the account.

If the e-mail exchange goes all right, set up an account with Yahoo! messenger and chat away—but don't give in to the temptation to tell him all about yourself too quickly. Don't tell him your children's names or where you work.

After a decent vetting period, you'll probably want to talk to him over the phone. Do not give out your home phone number or your cell.

 Buy a prepaid phone, register it to Minnie Mouse, and call him with that.

If he turns out to be a lunatic, a freak, or a Commie, you can change the number in a matter of minutes. You won't have to worry about persistent calls and e-mails and texts. And you won't need to worry that the next time you head to the grocery store, he'll be there, hiding behind a tower of bananas, ogling your melons (the ones in your basket, of course).

TIP: USE MELISSADATA

The site www.MelissaData.com is the best place to go if you're doing due diligence on a date. Click "Lookups" at the top of the home page.

You can run an astounding number of checks on this site, many of them for free: names and mailing addresses associated with an e-mail address; reverse phone lookups; businesses and roommates associated with a particular individual; campaign contributions by address; even the assessed value of someone's house.

When you've talked on the phone a couple of times, it will finally be time to meet. Whether you're heading to Starbucks or to miniature golf, be smart. Meet him there. Park a block or two away so he doesn't see you getting out of your car. Remember:

 If he's a stalker, your license plate number will tell him everything he needs to know about where you live.

If all goes well, he'll let you win at golf and buy you a sandwich at Chopper's Deli. Big spender. If you enjoy yourself, it's all good. But you're not quite out of the woods yet.

It's time to do a little due diligence on your prince. Look for warning signs that he's a frog. If he does not tell you where he lives, he is either Frank M. Ahearn or he is married. If he only meets you at particular times in particular places, he is married. If his e-mails and texts arrive at the same time every day, he is married. If you think or feel that he is married—guess what. He's married.

 Whether or not he's giving you a strange feeling, look him up on a people-finding service.

Most of these sites will give you a person's age, location, and relatives' names for free, and you can be fairly certain that they're accurate. If he says he's thirty-five, and they say he's forty-five, he's a lousy SOB.

Phone numbers usually come up on these searches, too. If you find one, give it a ringy dingy from a public or prepaid phone to see if a wife or kid picks up. Better yet, enter it into a site that offers reverse listings—i.e., the names and addresses associated with a given phone number. If you enter "reverse listings" in Google, you'll see about sixty of these Web sites. Take your pick and enter the number. Did he give you a real name? Is the landline registered to Mr. and Mrs. Adulterous Frog?

 Never pay for a reverse-listings check. Many Web sites offer this service for free, and the ones that charge you money are hoping you're too lazy to look for a free site.

If Mr. Frog has given you an address, use an online phone number and address reversal service like www.superpages.com to see if he's given you a real residential address or the location of a bar or mail drop.

If he gives you a phone number, find out if it's a cell phone or a landline. You can do this at www.localcallingguide.com. Pop in the area code and exchange, and the site will tell you if it is T-Mobile, Verizon, AT&T, and so on. If he told you it was his home number and it's a cell, or if the number comes up as a prepaid phone—danger, red lights, alarm. He is either broke, married, a criminal, or a hipster. Ugh.

As for e-mail: There is no one way to identify an e-mail account. Most services are free and anonymous these days. But you can try to get information by dropping the last part of the address—everything that comes after the @—and running the rest through a search engine. You might be surprised at what comes up: angry online screeds, Most Wanted lists, lots of stuff.

I hope that this solves everything, and that you're reading this chapter because you're about to start dating online and want to be prepared. If it's too late and you have a stalker on your hands, I'm sorry to hear that. But read on—I can still help you.

14

DISAPPEAR FROM A STALKER

IF YOU BELIEVE YOU'RE BEING STALKED, THERE'S ONE THING YOU should do immediately. I can't stress this enough:

 Contact your local police department and report it.

Your local police department can direct you to shelters, support groups, and other agencies and organizations that can help you right now. They've helped victims like you hundreds of times. If for any reason you have doubts or concerns about the local police—maybe your stalker is a police officer—contact the prosecutor's office or the police department in an adjacent precinct.

Law enforcement is on your side for this one. They can help you get a restraining order, and they're the only ones who can legally go after the bastard if he tries to hurt you.

But as we know, stalkers sometimes waltz right though restraining orders—and who cares if they're punished if you're not alive to see it? I read online that 20 percent of stalkers end up pulling a weapon on their victims. Some use them, and some just threaten to use them, but either way, let's hope it never gets to that point.

There are limits to what law enforcement can do. That's why you might choose to disappear and move to another neighborhood (or city, or country) for your own peace of mind. I've helped lots of people do just that, and in this chapter, I'll help you.

Here's principle No. 1:

 Assume the worst about any stalker.

That's the first thing I tell all my clients who are dealing with this problem. Your stalker might simply be pestering you with e-mails, phone calls, and unannounced visits right now. Maybe he's threatening you, but you don't think he'll ever act on it.

Take him seriously. Assume he's going to act. Assume he's going to break the law. You never know how a stalking situation is going to end, and a seemingly harmless encounter can very quickly become violent. For your own safety, I advise that you prepare for every possible outcome.

The types of stalkers I've dealt with fall into seven categories. All of them are dangerous and need to be avoided, but you'll need to tailor your reaction plan a little bit for each.

Rejected stalkers—the husbands, boyfriends, lovers, or platonic friends who don't want the relationship to end—are the most common type, and they are also the toughest to disappear from. They know a lot of your personal information, they've probably been to your home, and they've met your family and friends. These stalkers may have done a lot of snooping before the relationship ended, so you have to assume they know every piece of information that you left around the house, wrote in your diary, or confided in other friends.

Types of Stalkers

Rejected stalker: A former partner or friend who won't take "no" for an answer. You've told him you want him out of your life, and he's not listening.

Resentful stalker: An acquaintance or stranger motivated by the irrational belief that you've wronged him. Out for revenge.

Predatory stalker: A sexual criminal who's set his sights on you.

Intimacy seeker: An admirer who's convinced he or she is your soul mate.

Incompetent suitor: Someone who has a crush on you and wants a relationship but lacks social skills.

Erotomaniac: Someone who's convinced you're in love with him or her.

Cyber-stalkers: Any of the above, if they're stalking you primarily through the Internet.

You should also anticipate that a rejected stalker will go back to your family and friends in search of more information. Tell everyone you know that this individual is dangerous and no longer welcome in your life.

The other types of stalkers might not know you as well, but on the other side of that coin, you don't know *them* as well either. You don't know where they're likely to go to find more information about you. You don't know what will enrage them or give them false hope. You don't know whether they're going to snap and become violent, and you don't know if they're going to show up at your house in the middle of the night. Another online statistic I dug up: Four-fifths of stalkers use more than one way to stalk their victims. So you have to be nimble with them: Expect the unexpected.

Whichever type of stalker is after you, you need to do five things to get him out of your life: Change the way you communicate, change the way you handle your money, perform disinformation, change your location (if they know where you live), and change your life. I'll address each in turn.

CHANGE THE WAY YOU COMMUNICATE

Prepaid cell phones are going to be your most valuable tool. Go to an off-brand phone retailer (so your name isn't in the books of those big, national, easily pretextable companies) and get as many prepaid phones as possible. Buy one for every room of your house if you can, and leave the same voice-mail message on each: "Hi, my name is _____ and I am a stalking victim. I live at (your address), and I use this phone for emergencies only. If you're listening to this message, please send help." That way, if your stalker attacks you at home and manages to snatch your phone out of your hand, a dispatcher will know exactly what's going on.

Buy two more prepaid phones for nonemergency personal calls. Pay for all of your phones with cash; tear up and dump the receipts in a public trash can. Use one of your phones for incoming calls and the other for outgoing calls. Ask your family and friends to use prepaid cell phones to call you if it's at all possible.

Change your phones and phone numbers frequently by taking the SIM cards out of your phones, flushing them, and dumping the phones themselves in trash cans far from your house.

Stop using your old cell phone, but don't disconnect it, especially if your stalker is calling you up and leaving threatening messages. If he finds out you've disconnected your old phone number, he'll try to find your new one. Let him leave those long, crazy messages. Record them as evidence for the police.

Another tool you can use when you're making phone calls is a spoof card, which changes the way your number appears on a person's caller ID. Use this if you have a rejected stalker and you suspect the person you're calling might report your phone number to him. If the person you've called dials *69 after you've called with a spoof card, the recording will state the bogus number. Some *69 services allow people to press a button and connect to the number that just dialed them, and sure enough, if someone does this to you when you've called with a spoof card, he'll get the bogus number you programmed.

BE CAREFUL WITH TOLL-FREE NUMBERS

When you dial a toll-free number, even if you have a private or restricted number, your phone number shows up on its caller ID. Use a spoof card to call *all* toll-free numbers.

You need to change the way you e-mail, too. This isn't new advice, but it works: Go on Gmail or another free and anonymous service that allows you to save draft e-mails. Share the password with your closest loved ones, and communicate by saving but not sending the drafts. Only access the Internet from free public wireless or by buying a prepaid air card from a cellular carrier.

Your Internet presence should be a particular concern if you have a cyber-stalker. Make sure you've wiped up all your digital footprints using the techniques I described in the "Misinformation" chapter. In particular, get off of social networking Web sites and ask your friends and family to detag and delete their photographs of you. Needless to say, they should "unfriend" your stalker, too, if he's an acquaintance.

Before you get off of social media, send a note to all your friends and acquaintances letting them know you're being stalked. Tell them

---

THE FACE OF A CYBER-STALKER

One headline that caught my eye recently involved the story of Steve Phillips, an ESPN sportscaster whose twenty-two-year-old mistress turned psycho and began to stalk his wife and fourteen-year-old son. She posed as one of his son's high school classmates on an instant-messaging service and sent him messages asking personal questions about his parents' marriage. Then she tried to add him as a friend on Facebook.

From what I've read in the son's police statement, it's obvious that she managed to get a lot of information out of him before he became suspicious, even though he found her questions aggressive and strange.

The moral of the story is: If your friends and family don't know you have a stalker, they're not going to realize they're giving all your personal information to a predator. Keep them in the know!

---

not to give your information to anyone who asks for it, and request that they notify the police detective on your case if anyone tries.

Finally, it's time to change your snail mail. You don't want your stalker to be able to come over and grab your mail from the box. Obtain a few private mailboxes in your town: one to replace your home mailbox and another as a storage box for your cell phones, prepaid credit cards, and all the other documents you're going to need to evade your stalker.

Now that you have a secure place for your bills to go, you're ready to change your credit card and bank account information.

CHANGE THE WAY YOU HANDLE YOUR MONEY

Contact your credit card companies and change your billing address to one of your new mailboxes. If you can, don't get paper bills at all;

opt for online billing, but be sure to change the mailing address your company has on file.

The company is going to want a phone number, too, and I recommend you provide one for a police station or a women's shelter. A police number will make a skip tracer think you're a cop. A women's shelter will alert any decent skip tracer that something's fishy about his client's story. Either way, let's hope the skip tracer backs off the search.

When you contact your credit card company to change your information, mention that you're the victim of a stalker. Ask the company to confirm all of your details before it releases any information over the phone. To make sure the rep gets the message, be extreme: say your stalker has tried to kill you, even if he hasn't.

FRANK'S PHILOSOPHY

It's OK to exaggerate when you're in danger.

The credit card company might offer to put some additional security on your account, such as sending a text to your cell phone every time someone uses your card. Don't do this. If your stalker penetrates your cell phone account, he might configure his own phone so that he intercepts your text messages. If that happens, he'll know where you are based on what you're buying.

Change your banking information next. Call your banks and change your mailing address and phone number—once again using a mail drop and a number for a police station. If your stalker knows where you work, get direct deposit so you don't have to show up at a bank branch to cash your paychecks. If he *doesn't* know where you work, do something different when cashing your checks, since you don't want to give him the chance to pretext your bank and figure out the name of your employer. Cash your check at a check-cashing store and then deposit your money in an ATM that's nowhere near your office or your home.

If possible, avoid the bank altogether. Get a prepaid Visa or MasterCard or a gift card, and load it up in a retail or convenience store.

PERFORM DISINFORMATION

If your stalker knows where you live, you might be considering a move. I think this is a great idea. But before you go, I encourage you to protect yourself with the techniques I described in my "Disinformation" chapter.

Create as many bogus trails as you can for your stalker to follow. While he's off following them, you'll have a chance to build your new life at your leisure.

I've seen disinformation save countless lives. One of those lives belonged to a client of mine we'll call Dana. Dana was a small business owner whose online advertisements attracted the attention of a stalker. As the stalker's threats grew scarier and scarier, Dana decided that she wanted to pick up and move. She told me that the tedium and sacrifice of disappearing would be worth it if she never had to deal with this guy again.

The trouble with Dana's stalker was that he had plenty of money and had already spent thousands of dollars on private investigators to track her down. This guy was very rich and very deranged. That meant she couldn't just delete her personal information from the phone book and buy a new house. She had to go for the full-court press of misinformation, relocation—and thorough disinformation.

We spent a few days going through all of Dana's public records, deleting them where we could. We called up her phone and utility companies and told them they got her name wrong; she was actually called "Donna." We changed all the addresses and phone numbers associated with her accounts to the contact information of a local women's shelter, lining her trail with red flags for a scrupulous investigator to see.

Next, we sat down and thought about the kind of private investigator that we knew Dana's stalker was going to hire. The stalker was wealthy enough that if one investigator objected or refused to do an illegal search, he'd simply fire that investigator and hire another and another until he found one who'd do whatever he asked, including break the law.

We therefore had to be prepared for someone doing every kind of search, legal and illegal, for Dana: DMV records, credit reports, phone and cell histories, bank statements, health records, and credit card transactions. Most private investigators wouldn't touch searches like these, but it's amazing how much pull a Ben Franklin has over some other people.

As you know, disinformation has three parts: hook, line, and sinker. We decided that for our hook we would lead Dana's pursuers to Ypsilanti, Michigan. From there, we were going to seriously fuck with their heads.

Dana traveled to Ypsilanti personally. She paid for her plane ticket with cash. If her stalker had hired a *really* good private investigator, he would smell a rat if he saw that plane ticket on her credit card. We had to appear to be covering our tracks.

Once in Ypsilanti, the first thing she did was look at apartments. She expressed interest in one, and a real estate agent handed her a flyer with more information, including the apartment's address. Later that afternoon, the real estate agent ran a credit check on her—the first false clue for the PI to find.

Dana wandered back to her rental car and shut the door. She grabbed her cell phone and dialed a number I'd written down on a slip of paper for her—the local electric company. Her conversation went something like this:

DANA: *Hi, this is Dana Rickie. I'm about to move to an apartment, and I need to get electric service there, please.*

REPRESENTATIVE: *Sure! What is your address?*

DANA [reading off the flyer]: *It's 850 West Cross Street, Apartment ---, Ypsilanti, Michigan, 48197.*

REPRESENTATIVE: *Great.*

DANA: *I'd like my bills sent to my office, please.*

REPRESENTATIVE: *Sure. What is your address?*

DANA read off a bogus address.

REPRESENTATIVE: *Thanks. Do you have a contact number we could put on your account?*

DANA gave her the phone number of a local women's shelter.

REPRESENTATIVE: *Thank you. Welcome.*

Dana and the representative hung up. She hoped that the utility company would run a credit check on her, leaving another cookie crumb for the PI to follow.

Next, Dana dialed the phone company and asked for landline service to her new apartment. Again, she gave a bogus address for billing, and this time the contact number she gave was for the local gun club. Another red flag for the PI to question. The phone company read out what her new phone number was going to be and thanked her for her business.

The next number Dana dialed was for cable TV. She gave the address of her "apartment," and for her contact number, she used the number she had just been given by the phone company.

Dana had now set up all the services she needed for a home. Of course, she never moved into the apartment or called the real estate agent to say she was no longer interested. Nor did she cancel the phone, electric, or cable order. Those accounts were going to be around for a few months: incomplete orders with contact numbers and billing addresses on file. They were perfect bait for her stalker's hired goons.

Dana turned her key in the ignition and drove to a bank a few miles away. While waiting in line at the bank, she looked around for a little sign confirming that the bank used a search service to check on potential customers' overdraft histories. Yes, there it was. She smiled.

Once she got to the window, she asked to speak with the branch manager about opening up a checking account. He was happy to oblige. She knew that he was going to run her name through the search service to see if she had overdrafts at any other banks. It was highly illegal for anyone to pretext those search services, but she knew her stalker would find a private investigator who didn't care about that kind of thing. He'd find out about this checking account, and he'd be even more convinced that she'd moved to Ypsilanti.

At the end of the meeting, Dana asked for an ATM card and had it mailed to a private mail drop. With her temporary checkbook in hand, she hit the local supermarket and got a supermarket card, too. She opened up every kind of account she could possibly need to live in Ypsilanti. Once her ATM card came, she opened up a video store account and an account at the local bookstore, using the address of "her" Ypsilanti apartment. No stone was left unturned.

Eventually, Dana flew back to her hometown and got ready to relocate for real. But she could do so at her leisure, because her stalker and his cronies were tied up trying to find her in Ypsilanti. She never had to pay for any of the utilities she signed up for, because technicians came to the apartment, discovered no one lived there, and canceled the orders. Dana took off for an undisclosed location, and at my instruction her mother and sister called Realtors, restaurants, and apartment complexes in Ypsilanti and several other American cities for months afterward. If the PI got hold of their phone records, he probably cried in frustration.

Dana's family members were also happy to make calls to women's shelters and various types of help lines. We gave that stalker's private investigators every chance to realize that they were working with a criminal. With any luck, some of them went back to their client with his papers and shoved them up his nose, or some other dark place.

Dana is still safe today. Her stalker eventually gave up the search.

 **Disinformation works.**

If you are the subject of a persistent and potentially violent stalker, and have or can borrow the money to perform the kind of thorough disinformation Dana did, please do.

CHANGE YOUR LOCATION

Once you've covered your tracks and misled your pursuers, it will be time to find someplace new to live. With any luck, your stalker won't follow you.

 The safest way to move is by setting up a corporation and convincing your new landlord to write the lease in the corporation's name.

Put utilities and cable in the name of the corporation, and if the companies ask for a name, deviate from the way you spell it and give them a bogus contact number.

While you're at it, transfer the title of your car to your new corporation. Register your car and car insurance to the address of your private mail drop. If you don't own your car outright and are paying off a loan, change the address you have on file for that loan to a private mail drop. Never visit the mail drop where you send information about your car. Just get the people who own the mail drop to forward whatever you need to a different mail drop. Why? Motor vehicle records and car loan information are both very easy to get via pretext, so they're a major vulnerability for you.

On moving day, I suggest you keep tabs on your stalker at all times:

 Hire a private investigator to conduct surveillance on your stalker.

If you can afford it, hire a second investigator to shadow you at your location and see if anyone is watching you move. If your stalker isn't there personally, it's possible he's sent a representative.

Disconnect your phone, electric, and cable services at your old home, and buy new accounts from completely different companies at your new home. Do not create a "move order" to transfer your utilities to a new location. A good skip tracer can easily pretext a move order.

Cancel all your magazine subscriptions. Do not reorder them at your new location. Subscriptions are going to be one of your biggest vulnerabilities, especially if you're dealing with a Rejected Stalker who knows what you like to read. Pick up magazines at the newsstand when you're at 7-Eleven charging up your prepaid phone.

CHANGE YOUR LIFE

Once you've safely moved to your new location—or just made yourself less conspicuous where you are—you're going to have to build your new life very carefully. Your first step should be to introduce yourself to your neighbors and make them aware that you are being stalked. If you have photos of the stalker, distribute them widely, and if you have an order of protection, distribute that, too. Tell them that if they see the stalker snooping, they should contact the police as soon as possible.

Give photos of your stalker and your protection order to all your friends and family, too. If you have children, give these documents to their school, teachers, and day-care providers. The more good people you make aware of your problem, the safer you'll be.

Next, have a member of your local police department come over and do a "safety check" on your home. The officer will be able to tell you where your vulnerabilities lie.

If you live in an apartment complex and your manager has access to your apartment, explain your situation and ask him never to bring a repairperson or anyone else into your home without your permission. Supply the manager with photos and your protection order, and request that he be on the lookout.

Never throw subscription magazines, newspapers, bills, or other identifying information into your trash can. If you have a garage, use it at all times and keep it clean and uncluttered, so an attacker can't hide behind stacks of boxes or old machinery. Better yet, install a panic alarm in your garage that you can hit if a stalker runs in after you as you close the garage door.

If you have health insurance and need to go to the doctor, dentist, therapist, or any other medical professional, it's best to find one a few towns away. Your insurance records might give away your location. Pick up your prescriptions at small, mom-and-pop-type pharmacies, ideally also several towns away. I know it's a hassle, but:

 The layers you create between your activities and your location can make the difference between life and death.

If you plan to go on vacation, don't use an easily traceable frequent-flier account. You might have some miles left on an old account, but you have to ditch them. Give them to a family member, friend, or someone across the country with the same name as you.

Renting a car? Under no circumstance should you give your correct phone number to the car rental agent. Car rental companies bring up accounts via phone numbers, and they were always my first stop when I had to locate a person who was traveling. I'd pretext the car rental companies with the subject's phone number, and before

I knew it, I'd have all her information, including flight and hotel details. Those are other pieces of information you should *never* give a car rental company, even if it asks. Make something up.

FRANK'S PHILOSOPHY

If you fear for your safety, when in doubt, lie.

If you belong to any supermarket discount clubs, change the spelling of your name and the address associated with your membership, and then stop using it. A private investigator might be able to find out where you shop or even get some banking information from that account.

Don't buy anything from any mail order companies, but if it is imperative you do so for some reason, use a prepaid credit card, deviate from the spelling of your name on the order, and ship your order to your mail drop.

PERSONAL SECURITY

Regardless of whether or not you've decided to move, you should make your home and surroundings as secure as possible. Get an alarm for your home and set up a camera system. If you use a computer at work, ask your security provider and your boss to set up a live webcam system you can monitor all day.

If your office has a security department, make the security director aware of your problem. Alert your supervisor and coworkers, too, if possible. Circulate a picture of your stalker and tell everyone you work with not to share *any* details about your activities or schedule over the phone.

Change your routine frequently. Never commute to and from work the same way two times consecutively. If you bike, jog, or walk, use different routes every day, and make sure they're always crowded and well-lit. For added safety, exercise and commute with a partner.

Concentrate on finding ways to document every encounter with your stalker. If your stalker has threatened or committed acts against you and you haven't been able to record the incidents, you should still go to the local precinct, sit with a detective, and let the police know what's going on. If they can't make a move on your stalker, at least they'll be aware of him—and patrol cars can keep a more careful watch on your house.

If you've tried changing your phone number and the stalker keeps finding it, it's possible the stalker is using an investigative agency to obtain his information. Use Google to find each state's private detective association and e-mail them asking if they will forward the following note to their members:

URGENT

My name is _____. I am being stalked by an individual who keeps hiring private investigators to track me down and obtain my personal information. If this person comes to you, please report the incident to [the name of your local police detective] as soon as possible. This is a matter of life and death. Thank you.

Most private investigators will heed this message and assist you if your stalker contacts them.

I used to work with private investigators all the time, helping them locate people, and when they gave me a name, it was not uncommon for me to recognize the signs of a stalking situation. When I saw those signs, I'd alert the private investigator and not pursue the skip trace. Like clockwork, another private investigator would contact me with the same request an hour later. Most private investigators will immediately terminate a working relationship with someone they believe is a stalker.

Every time your stalker confronts you, seek help if you can. But know how to defend yourself for those times you can't. Find a local self-defense class and take a course. If you cannot afford to take classes, go to the local karate school and explain your situation to the teacher. Most will assist you and at least give you a few basic moves. Keep in mind the old skip tracer's saying that every no leads to a yes—if one person doesn't help, the next one very well might. Don't be discouraged. Keep trying places and keep asking.

Do not be afraid to ask people for help. I always helped stalking victims for minimal or no cost, and plenty of other people will do the same, including locksmiths, security contractors, and private investigators.

If you find suspicious packages at your doorstep or in the mail, do not hesitate to contact the police. It is better to be safe than sorry, and if the police are familiar with your situation, they'll understand perfectly. If someone contacts you on the phone claiming to be from your bank, credit card company, or the IRS, do not give out any information. Do not acknowledge that it is you on the phone. Get a call-back number and as much information as possible and tell the representative that "someone" will call back. Then surf the net and see if the number is online, or ask a friendly private investigator to find information on the phone number given.

THINGS TO KEEP IN MIND

Antistalking experts agree that, unfortunately, there is no single course of action that will end your nightmare or make you completely safe. But the experts and victims I've talked to all agree that the following safety tips are essential:

 Stalkers crave attention, so never confront or yell at them. Never send a friend or a family member to talk to them, either. This is law enforcement's job.

 Never open your front door unless you know who is on the other side and you feel completely safe.

 If your keys go missing—even if you think you've just misplaced them—change your locks immediately.

 Web sites change, so use the search term "stalking assistance" in any search engine for sites that can provide you with more information on how to deal with your stalking or abusive situation. You can also contact the National Center for Victims of Crime at (202) 467-8700 or visit the center's Web site at www.ncvc.org.

Good luck to you.

15

DISAPPEAR FROM THE COUNTRY

> Freedom is not merely the opportunity to do as one pleases; neither is it merely the opportunity to choose between set alternatives. Freedom is, first of all, the chance to formulate the available choices, to argue over them—and then, the opportunity to choose.
>
> —*C. Wright Mills*

YOU KNOW THAT OLD SAYING, "WHEREVER YOU GO, THERE YOU ARE?" Well, some of us are fine with that as long as we're the only ones who come along for the ride.

Lots of people fantasize about ditching it all for the "palm tree lifestyle," as I call offshore living, but few follow through. They don't think it's achievable, or they imagine their problems will just follow them to their new home.

Offshore living is not just for the rich. It's achievable and fun. I've done it, and in this chapter, I'm going to show you how to do it, too. Whether you're leaving the country to protect your assets, cut your taxes, flee your pursuers, or just soak up some rays, I'll be able to help you.

The one thing I am not going to discuss is taxes. I've had my own unfortunate experiences with the Big Brothers who collect the dough, and I'm no tax expert. My suggestion is that when you finish this book, find a good tax attorney who can make your transition to the palm tree world an easy and legal one.

With that said ... let's roll!

WHAT KIND OF PEOPLE LIVE OFFSHORE?

Offshore living and banking have a pretty bad reputation. When I discuss offshore banking with inexperienced clients, they assume something shady about that world.

Everywhere you go on Earth, and in everything you do, you will find good and bad people. Yes, criminals and money launderers use offshore accounts. But so do independent thinkers, worldly adventurers, and staunch libertarians. I personally have found lots of noble and like-minded people in my adventures offshore.

The offshore world is the Wild West of disappearing. Its rules are constantly changing, and its people are some of the most interesting you'll ever meet. This lifestyle places a big emphasis on personal freedom— which means *you* choose whether to live honorably or not.

Do your homework by reading as much as you can about offshore living. Then make the right choice for you.

Before you commit to moving anywhere, I suggest you contact a professional to discuss which foreign countries are a good match for you. Look for a relocation company or a publication that helps people relocate to the country you like. (One of my favorites is Parler Paris, a Web site that offers all the information you need to relocate to the City of Lights. Check it out at www.parlerparis.com.)

Visit a country before you move there. Visiting seems like something only an idiot would fail to do, but I've heard too many horror stories from people who relocated on a dream and no research and ended up paying the price.

TIP ON TICKETS

When you travel to your new home, whether you're just doing some reconnaissance or you're making the big move, don't go there directly. Buy a ticket to a far-off airport, then another ticket to another airport, and then a ticket from there to your destination on the smallest, most Podunk airline you can find (within reasonable safety limits, of course). For maximum security, pay for each ticket with a different prepaid credit card and call airline companies directly on different prepaid cell phones to make the reservations.

Once you pick a country, hire a local lawyer to help you settle in if you can. Ask a friend or business associate in the country to recommend one, if possible. A lawyer will keep you from getting swindled by predatory salesmen if you're still learning a country's language and customs.

The first thing you're going to need after you land is a place to live. Personally, I would rent in a foreign country before I purchased property. Buyers, beware of those beachfront lots for sale at great prices. Sure, it's right on the beach, but can you build a house on that land? Can you get running water or utilities? Labor may be cheap in your new paradise, but supplies and shipping may not be. There's a reason the cost of living is so low in some countries.

Make sure you don't get swindled by local real estate agents. I know a person who purchased a condominium in Central America. It was a really nice place on the beach. He paid $80,000, which he thought was a great deal until he learned that the actual price of the place was eighty thousand in local currency—about 40 percent less than he paid.

Ask plenty of questions: Can you get Internet service at your new property? How fast is it? Does cellular service work in the area? What are the fees? Have a landline installed in your apartment as a backup in case cell service turns out to be unreliable.

What about garbage removal? Street cleaning? The basic services we take for granted are not always available in foreign countries.

Squatters can be a problem in your new country, so some people hire a caretaker or others to live in their house when they're not around. Before you purchase property, you should research area squatting laws.

The second issue you want to look into is medical care. Do some research into the doctors and hospitals in your country of choice to make sure that proper medical services are available. Basic care may be available, but certain major treatments may not be. What happens if you have a heart attack or some other devastating illness or injury? Where will you be taken?

Check with your insurance carrier about how living in a foreign country will affect your coverage. Look into area pharmacies. Do they carry your prescriptions? If not, is it legal to have your medicine shipped from the United States to this new country? Can you live without that medicine if you can't have it shipped?

What about dentists and eye doctors? Are they available? Chances are high that you're going to have at least some medical needs when you get to your new country. Even if you're in great shape, you'll be adjusting to the climate and food and germs and diseases of a new country. Inadequate medical care could turn your offshore dream into a terminal nightmare.

If you have children, what are you going to do for their education? If schools in your new country aren't up to par, are you willing to homeschool them? Have you put together all the resources that this will require? If good schools are near you, will they respect your family's wish for privacy and discretion? Don't compromise your children's future. Make sure your new home is a good fit for them, too.

If you're convinced that you can get adequate medical care and services for your family where you've chosen to live, the next topic to research is citizenship and legal residence. It is vital that you perform due diligence on your new home by investigating the country's tax structure, financial security, and political stability. How do you think these are going to change in the coming years? Is there likely to be political unrest or an economic spike or depression? The last thing you want to do is jump ship on your own country, only to discover yourself in the same type of place three years later.

Obtaining citizenship in some island countries is not very hard. Several countries that market themselves as offshore havens offer second passports if you are of a certain age and deposit a required amount of money through their banking system. Second passports may be cool to show your friends or impress a lady, but they're not going to be much help to you, especially if you're trying to live under the radar. After all the work you've done to minimize the amount of information that's out there on you, why would you want to *add* information to public records? I disapprove.

Now that you have your living situation taken care of, you'll need to figure out how you're going to support yourself. Whether you plan to live off of an existing income stream or a business, make sure you can manage your income virtually.

What you do to generate income is up to you. Maybe you just won a lawsuit or the lottery and you plan to live on that windfall. Maybe you liked your job in the States and want to continue working in the same field. Maybe you have plans to develop a new business— now's the time to go for that dream!

One client had always been fascinated by watches, and after expatriating to Madrid, he started selling them on eBay. He made thousands of dollars without ever touching the merchandise. Customers paid him anonymously via PayPal and sent him so many questions about his merchandise that he eventually decided to write an e-book about watches. Proceeds from this e-book nearly tripled his income. And no one ever knew he lived in Madrid.

Even a decade after the dot-com bust, there's still gold in them there Internets. You can make money hand over fist if you have the right attitude. Find a "push of the button"-type business that interests you and get busy.

Some countries—mostly tropical islands—will allow you to set up an **International Business Corporation (IBC),** which will enable you to open a bank account and conduct business in your home country without paying local taxes. These cost about $1,000 to open up in most countries and are an excellent way to live under the radar in your new home. You can register your apartment and bank account to this corporation, shielding your name and identity from international authorities and people prying into your accounts.

If you plan to start a Web site associated with your IBC, it would be wise to visit the company that will be hosting your Web site and observe its operations. When I had my Web site parked offshore, I had quite a few problems, mainly due to an understaffed tech support department.

Once you earn your money, how are you going to manage it? Banking will be your next concern, although I'm sure you're way ahead of me on that one. I'm going to take a leap of faith and assume that if you are smart enough to make your money, you are smart enough to know how to research a safe and secure bank. I banked offshore at one point in my career and encountered two problems: The bank I chose charged high fees on every transaction it conducted, and the checks I deposited took longer than average to clear. Eventually, I found a better bank to suit my needs.

Only you know the best way to handle your assets offshore. One option you might not have heard of before you left the country is the **digital currency** exchange. You will almost certainly come in contact with it during your offshore life.

Digital currency, n.: an international form of electronic money backed by gold or silver or some other account. Proponents such as the people at the London Gold Exchange tout it as "the future of online banking," but for now it is widely used for money laundering and other shady purposes.

I have mixed feelings about digital currency. The companies that offer it are all closely monitored by international authorities, and many have been closed down for illegal behavior. Big Brother views digital currency suspiciously and frowns on those who dabble in it. Who needs these headaches? I could think of twenty more reasons you shouldn't bother banking with digital currency, but you know your own financial situation better than anyone, so I'll leave the decision up to you.

All I can say is be careful to obey international law. Do you know what a **John Doe subpoena** is? If not, familiarize yourself with this term now.

> **John Doe subpoena, n.:** a court summons served to an individual whose identity is not known, such as an anonymous writer, blogger, or offshore banker. The IRS serves offshore banks with these subpoenas to find out the identities of their customers.

I got caught up in a John Doe subpoena when I banked offshore, and it was not fun. Make sure you're banking the legal way by contacting a lawyer or reading up on international tax law. Do not underestimate the tenacity or the reach of the IRS!

Living, citizenship, medicine, business, and banking: Once you hammer out those details, you'll be on your way to a full-on offshore lifestyle. You'll be joining an illustrious group of privacy-minded expatriates who sometimes call themselves "PTs." This acronym stands for many things, including Perpetual Tourist, Part-time Traveler, or Prior Taxpayer. If you search the Internet for information on offshore living, you'll probably see this term come up frequently.

People who embrace the PT lifestyle value personal liberty and private property and generally have a deep distrust of all things government—my kind of people. When the IRS was auditing me, I came to understand that the money I earned in the United States was truly not mine, since I was accountable to an entity that called all the shots. It was an eye-opening experience and gave me newfound respect for the people who find a way to take back control of their lives and money without violating a single law.

PTs talk a lot about "living the Flags." They're referring to two theories about living your life offshore with minimal government intrusion. These are the Three Flag Theory, popularized in the sixties by an investment guru named Harry Schultz, and the Five Flag Theory, W. G. Hill's expanded version of the idea.

LIVING THE FLAGS

THE THREE FLAG THEORY

Harry Schultz wrote that you should seek an international home with the following three criteria in mind:

1. Citizenship

Your citizenship and passport should be in a country that does not tax income you make or create outside of its borders.

2. Business Base

Earn your money somewhere with low corporate taxes.

3. Live as a Tourist

Find a place with laws, business practices, and customs that share your values, a place where you can live and work legally in the manner you choose.

THE FIVE FLAG THEORY

W. G. Hill argued that you shouldn't commit to life in one country but rather spread your existence out over five countries to reduce government intrusion.

1. Citizenship

Have your citizenship and passport in a country that does not tax income you make or create outside of its borders.

2. Legal Residence

Simultaneously, establish legal residence in a country recognized as a tax haven. Speak with a tax attorney about how to do this.

3. Business Base

Earn your money in a country with low corporate taxes.

4. Asset Havens

Keep your money in a country with low taxes and strict privacy laws.

5. Playgrounds

Spend your money in a country with low value added tax (VAT) and consumption tax.

These are appealing theories, and the Internet abounds with advice on how to make them work for you. But before you run out and join the movement, take time to determine what is realistic for you as a person and your finances.

For me, Three Flags is more realistic and easier to manage. Very few people have time to shuttle back and forth between five countries every year. Plus, laws and tax policies in countries change all the time, so the life of a Five Flags follower is constantly in flux. I say nuts to that. Offshore living is supposed to be relaxing.

Offshore living is a wild ride. If you skip town and land in a different country, you'll meet rich guys, poor guys, criminals, heroes, intellectuals, morons, gamblers, cowboys, artists, businessmen, athletes, fat slobs, and just about every other type of character you can think of on your journey. The only people who can't make it in this world are the faint of heart. Bon voyage.

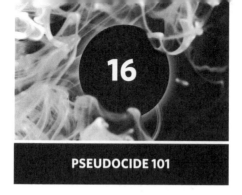

PSEUDOCIDE 101

I HAVE ALWAYS BEEN INTRIGUED WITH THE IDEA OF PSEUDOCIDE—to me, it's the ultimate disappearing act. Of course, it's super illegal and could land you in prison for years, yadda, yadda, yadda. But you have to admit, it's still pretty glamorous.

> **Pseudocide, n.:** A fake death, staged for the purposes of collecting insurance money and/or escaping to a new life.

Pseudocide runs deep in literature and Hollywood—everywhere from *Romeo and Juliet* to the 1983 movie *Eddie and the Cruisers*, about a rock star who fakes his own death, only to return to the stage. My favorite has got to be Earl Hickey from the TV series *My Name Is Earl*, who faked his death to escape a biker chick. I can sympathize.

As a teen, I was awed by the rumors of Jim Morrison passing his own grave in Père Lachaise Cemetery. There were also the stories about Elvis Presley flipping burgers in a greasy spoon on Route 66. Even Billy the Kid may have done it: Two men, Brushy Bill Roberts and John Miller, both claimed to be him years after his "death." And none of us who were kids in the '70s can forget "D. B. Cooper," the man who hijacked a 727, parachuted out the back end, and might or might not have died that rainy night over Washington State. Nine years later, a kid found a quarter of his ransom money rotting in a bag along a riverbank. Was it proof that Cooper had died on impact— or a genius pseudocidal ploy from the only man in American history who's managed to get away with an airline hijacking?

We'll never know the answer, I suppose, but four decades after the hijacking, our imaginations still run rampant. Did you know that one town in the Pacific Northwest still celebrates "Cooper Day" in his honor? I guess pseudocide is a great way to keep your memory alive, even if you have to pretend to be dead to do it.

I'M NOT SURE WHAT TO TELL YOU ABOUT PULLING OFF A SUCCESSFUL pseudocide. It's hard to say just how difficult it might be, because the only people we hear about are the ones who get caught. Who knows how many people have done it successfully?

I wish there were some secret society where all the successful pseudocides could meet, led by someone like Midas Mulligan or Guy Montag. Oh, to be a fly on the wall. Unfortunately, the only stories I know have unhappy endings.

Pseudocide is definitely a risky business. But I love to think about what it would take to pull it off, and I bet you're curious, too. So I'll think out loud.

Step one is obvious:

 Search to see if you've left any clues while you were planning your disappearance.

Look back and determine if any of your actions in the past can indicate that you have been planning to leave town. Did you surf the net and look at apartment rentals in New Zealand? Will your e-mail history reveal inquiries to offshore bank accounts in Gabon? Perhaps last year you took a trip to Fiji and looked at properties for sale, and each week you get e-mail updates about new sales.

The trail you left behind might lead pursuers down the road of your future. Pseudocide is a disappearing act like any other in that you have to prepare for all possible events, including one in which your pursuers figure out that you're not really dead and start looking for you. If that happens, you're going to want to make sure you haven't left an obvious trail for them to follow.

Look at where your tracks lead:

 Contact your Internet service provider and request a copy of the addresses you visited and determine if your past can be connected to your future.

If it can, you need to revamp your exit plan.

Do the same with your telephone company and cell phone company. Review the numbers you've called, and if there is a connection to the future, revamp the plan. Go to the Seychelles if you've called the Bahamas. Fly to El Salvador if you've called about flights to Marrakech.

Where you're planning to go matters:

 You're going to get busted if you stay in the country.

It will only be a matter of time before the feds smell a rat. Leave the country. Select a small, ocean-and-palm-tree country that doesn't extradite criminals. Then, if you are busted, at least you have a fighting chance of not being returned to dance for the judicial band.

What are you going to do to build your new life once you're abroad? I guess it is safe to say:

 You'll need a new identity to pull off your caper.

This is where it gets tricky: Where and how does one obtain a new identity? Personally, I would attempt to obtain the identity of a person who lives in a different country from my own. I would also visit a small country where poverty runs deep and make a deal with a family man or woman to send that person a couple of thousand dollars every year for the use of his or her identifiers.

I would not buy an identity from someone selling false documents. False documents have ID numbers on them, and you probably do not know how to validate them or make sure the ID numbers are correct. For all you know, the forger could have used the same number on several passports or printed up fifteen passports in the name of Kyle Dowling. Imagine you and fourteen other Kyle Dowlings showing up on the same flight—highly unlikely, but not impossible.

I would also not buy an identity from someone who was selling duplicated documents. You have no clue if the information is still valid. You don't know if the person named on the documents is dead, alive, or in prison. Also, if you obtain someone else's information, your time is limited because the documents need to be renewed. If the subject of the duplicate ID dies, you are walking around with a dead man's identity: big problem.

Finally, if the person who sold you the new identity gets busted, he may roll over on you. Also a big problem. I'm telling you—the best route is to find a "friend" in a third world country and make that person's life a lot better by enlisting his or her help in applying for documents.

So what's the perfect time for pseudocide? I don't have a good answer for that, but I know when you shouldn't make the attempt.

 Don't try to tie your "death" to some natural or man-made disaster.

Insurance companies and law enforcement are well on top of that game.

Facing a passport-fraud charge in Hawaii, a man named Steven Chin Leung posed as his nonexistent brother, claiming that Steven was working at Cantor Fitzgerald during the September 11, 2001, attack on the World Trade Center. Steven walked away with a four-year sentence. Scratch the disaster idea.

If you want to fake your own death for the insurance money, you're going to need a partner in crime.

 Your loved ones will have to be in on the scheme.

Someone has to be there to collect the check. Of course, the more people you let in on a scheme, the more likely it is to fail.

It appears that a marital rift led to the spectacular failure of John Darwin, perhaps the most famous pseudocide in recent memory. Darwin, a British man with a wife and two grown children, paddled out to sea in his trusty canoe one afternoon in 2002 and never returned home for dinner. His wife, Anne, contacted the authorities and they executed a search, but it appeared John was fish food.

John contacted the lovely Mrs. Darwin and told her the truth shortly thereafter. But that didn't stop her from filing her claim with his insurance companies and receiving a reasonable chunk of change.

After a year or so lying low at his home, John obtained a new passport under the name of John Jones—a very clever move, considering the name would be lost in a sea of John Joneses. It was also smart of him to keep the first name he was born with instead of Jimmy, Chris, or Barney.

While among the dead, John was a busy man. He ran into an old friend, who mentioned that he had heard John was dead. John asked the man to remain quiet, which he did. When questioned by the authorities, the man stated that he just didn't want to get involved, even so far as to make an anonymous call. God bless him.

John also found himself a girlfriend in Kansas. That was fatal mistake No. 1 while his wife was still in the picture.

After a couple of years wandering the world and shopping for boats, John made his way to Panama while Anne sold the marital home. Together they purchased a two-bedroom condominium and a $350,000 tropical estate in Escobal. They intended to build a canoeing resort. That was fatal mistake No. 2. If they had read *How to Disappear,* they would know as you do now that disappearing necessitates a lifestyle change. After you disappear, your passions become your pitfalls.

In December 2007, John flew back to the United Kingdom with the intention of seeing his son but walked into a London police station claiming to have no memory of where he had been for the past

THANK YOU, JOHN DARWIN

Even though I have not met John Darwin as of this writing, I want to thank him from the bottom of my heart. When his story hit the news, practically every media outlet in the U.K. as well as several other countries contacted me, and all the media exposure skyrocketed my business to the forefront of the disappearing and privacy industry. The funny thing is that I spent twenty years hunting people down from Iowa to Helsinki, and no one cared. Then some mild-mannered Brit faked his death, and boom, there I am in the spotlight. John, if you ever read this: in the great words of Elvis, thank you, thank you, thank you.

About a year into John's sentence, I wrote him a letter introducing myself, telling him about my business, and asking if I could set up a meeting and visit him in the big house. A month later, I got a call from a guy with a British accent phoning from a Florida number. The gent introduced himself and told me that he was John's cellmate and John had asked him to contact me. He offered me the rights to John Darwin's life story for $250,000. I asked if he had a contract with John. He said he did. It was scribbled on a napkin.

I told him to screw off. But before he left me alone, he called me one last time claiming he could get real passports from the U.K. I hung up, and we never spoke again.

few years. My guess is that he wanted out of his marriage and the situation in Panama, and some malfunctioning part of his brain told him this was the way to do it. Anne expressed her joy on the return of her husband. Then someone typed in "John" "Anne" and "Panama" in Google and located a photo of the happy couple posted on their condominium Web site.

John wasn't a pseudocide hero after all. He was just a dumb crook. This was a near perfect crime and practically a perfect case of pseudocide. Rumor has it that the couple had marital troubles. I guess Anne didn't mind committing a huge felony with her husband, but sharing him with a girlfriend in Kansas was out of the question.

I hope John's mistakes are obvious to you. What kind of buffoon walks into a police station claiming five and a half years of amnesia only three months after his wife relocates to Panama? The felonious couple was sentenced to six-year vacations each, compliments of her majesty the Queen of England.

Darwin was the forerunner of a pseudocide trend in the world of disappearing. Pseudocide has become a fashionable thing to attempt in the wake of the global recession, and every CEO who flames out spectacularly in his attempt to flee the country teaches us another lesson about faking your own death successfully.

The star of my Pseudocide Book of Shame has to be Marc Schrenker, CEO of some financial joint, who was served a slew of subpoenas on his home and business by the feds. Marc knew the jig was up. He decided to fly off in his plane, call Mayday, set the auto-pilot, and bail out with his parachute.

What a totally cowardly thing to do. He could have killed dozens of people. Can we all agree on this?

 Pseudocide is illegal, but it's especially not OK if you're putting other people's lives in danger.

After the flying scam man landed safely on the ground, he hitched a ride to a police station claiming that he had been in a canoeing accident. How ironic. The police were kind enough to take him to a local motel for the night, and the next morning, Marc fled on foot to a storage facility where he had stashed his motorcycle and other supplies.

He hit the open road and found refuge at a campground in Quincy, Florida. The backstory he told the groundspeople was that he and his friends were traveling cross-country. Marc paid in cash and got himself a tent, firewood, Internet service, and a six-pack of Bud.

That night, he e-mailed a friend—an amazingly stupid move— claiming that the accident was a mistake and that he was too embarrassed to come forward. Then he said he would be gone by the time the friend read the e-mail.

He was in police custody the following day. The owner of the campground grew suspicious when Marc did not check out. He approached Marc's tent and saw a red stain: blood. Coincidentally, not long after that, the sheriff's department contacted different business owners in the area asking if anything unusual had happened.

The owner of the campground volunteered that a tent in his campground had a big red bloodstain on it. The sheriff's department swarmed the area. Marc had several cuts on his wrist and had lost a significant amount of blood. He was airlifted to a hospital.

Another lesson for us would-be disappearing artists:

 Don't commit pseudocide if it's going to make you want to commit *real* suicide!

Marc now had to face the music from Florida, Alabama, Indiana, and possibly the United States Coast Guard and the Federal Aviation Administration. Instead of crashing his plane, why didn't he just let someone else fly him to a country that doesn't extradite criminals? Somewhere like Nigeria would have welcomed him and his millions of dollars. I think he has some mental health problems.

CEO PSEUDOCIDE?

One question that a lot of readers e-mail me is about Ken Lay from Enron. Do I think he faked his death? No comment!

You don't have to be as dumb as Marc to get busted for pseudocide. If you choose to fake your death, it is essential that you remain convincing in every little detail—more so than with any other type of disappearing. Remember:

 The slightest oddity in your story will get you busted.

John Stonehouse, a onetime member of the British Parliament, knew that all too well. Imagine—a politician disappearing. If only some of our politicians would follow suit.

In November 1974, Stonehouse left his clothing on a Miami beach and was presumed dead, but he was secretly flying to Australia with his mistress. While setting up shop, he had funds wired in one name and deposited in another, which caught the attention of a snoopy bank teller. She reported the curiosity to the law, which decided to look into the activities of this mysterious Brit.

The police suspected Stonehouse of being Lord Lucan, who had recently fled the United Kingdom after the murder of his children's nanny. Now that's what I call the Fluke Factor! Mr. Stonehouse was searching for the good life with his young filly, but a case that had nothing to do with him screwed up life in paradise.

On Christmas Eve, a little more than a month after his great escape from Miami, Stonehouse was in custody. He was sentenced to seven years in prison but only served four. Afterward, he married his mistress, wrote several novels, and became a local celebrity.

As for Lord Lucan, he has been spotted many places in the world, just like Carmen Sandiego. The only difference is that the good Lord is still out there on the run.

People who commit pseudocide want to make like Lord Lucan and disappear successfully. Some people, such as Patrick McDermott, have come tantalizingly close. McDermott disappeared from a fishing expedition in 2005, leaving all of his possessions in his cabin. He was in financial trouble at the time.

But as I told you earlier, an investigative team hired to find Patrick set up the Web site findpatrickmcdermott.com and was interested to see that the site got a bunch of hits in Acapulco. The investigators did a little poking around the area and met more than a dozen witnesses who said they'd seen Patrick.

As the investigators zeroed in on their prey, Patrick sent a message through a "representative": Leave me alone. Eventually they found out that he was working on the crew of a yacht under the name Patrick Kim. He's probably going to have to face the music from authorities.

Too bad.

17

FINAL THOUGHTS

DISAPPEARING IS HARD. IT'S TEDIOUS. IT CAN BE DANGEROUS AND demanding. It requires cash, energy, sacrifice, rigorous thinking, courage, and determination. You'll have to be a perfectionist. You'll have to pay attention to every little detail. But guess what? If you're not a complete whack job, you've got an advantage over three-quarters of the people out there who are trying to disappear. I'm constantly amazed by the level of craziness I encounter every day in my line of work.

In this last chapter, I'll leave you with some parting thoughts on what to expect in the wide world of the disappeared. None of this is really essential knowledge, but I hope it will be of some use. It never hurts to be prepared. Think of me as Uncle Frank wishing you out the door on your way to a freer, more private life.

Here's the first of my final lessons:

You'll meet a lot of crazies in the land of the disappeared.

I meet dozens of them every day. One was a woman I'll call Crazy Jane.

I was sitting in my office one day when a client called me and asked if it was possible to teach someone how to disappear. My answer was yes, of course, so he asked me how. He wanted me to give him a checklist of things to do. I told him it all depends on the budget, needs, and goals of the person who's disappearing.

A few days later, he called again, and he asked if I would meet with his client to discuss teaching her how to disappear. I agreed. We set a meeting for the following week. I figured we would meet, have coffee, and chat away, or they'd buy me dinner.

Wrong!

My client told me the general area where we would be meeting. That evening, I made my way there. After a few minutes, I got a call: They were at a nearby motel. I was to meet them in their room. Uh, OK, I thought.

In the room, I was greeted by my client and a woman with an accent named Jane. After we got the formalities out of the way, she told me her story. She was independently wealthy and a passionate animal-rights activist. She told me she had brought lawsuits against several animal farms, resulting in jail time for the abusers. I asked her to clarify exactly who, what, and where, promising her I wouldn't judge. She refused and left it at that.

Jane said people were making threats on her life. They had been leaving dead chickens and slaughtered calves on her property. My client interrupted and said a pipe bomb was found on Jane's property as well.

Jane said she took all of these threats seriously. "As you should," I replied. I asked about her financial situation and how she planned to make a living once she disappeared. She explained that she was from a wealthy European family that ran a family company. She was living off her trust from the company and was divorced, so money was no problem.

As I sat listening to this woman, the first thought in my head was, *She is rather calm about this*. She talked as if she were telling me things she thought about, not things she actually experienced. I probed more. I asked to see her wallet, and she flat out said no. I asked to see only her driver's license, and she said no. Finally, I asked for her Social Security number. She refused. Considering this woman wanted my help, she was not being too cooperative.

I expressed my concerns with the situation and wanted her to explain why she was being so defiant. Her explanation was that she worked for the government—work of some kind that made absolutely no sense to me. She had a top-secret security clearance, and the government had issued her a fake identity.

Here's an important lesson I have learned over the years from people like Jane:

 **When things get elaborate, get cautious.**

You know you're dealing with crazies when they start talking about "castles" and "top-secret clearance" in the same breath. Jane revealed more stories of growing up among royalty, having servants, and so forth. In her conversation, she mentioned a town in the United Kingdom where I had been several times. I made an open-ended comment about the town that should have prompted some type of response. She ignored my statement, making me think she had never been there.

The nutshell of our conversation was that she was rich and wanted to move so the animal people couldn't find and kill her. The meeting ended on a cordial note, and both parties stated we'd be in touch.

My client walked me to my car, and before he spoke, I said, "She's full of shit!" He disagreed. He tried to convince me she was the real thing. He saw dollar signs, but I saw trouble. The meeting had made me very uncomfortable.

I had enough experience with people to know she was not from the state we met in, so I drove around the motel parking lot looking for a car with out-of-state tags. There was no such car in the lot. It was an isolated area, so I drove to the diner down the road. There I found a car bearing Pennsylvania tags and copied down the number.

Next day in the office, I had someone run the license plate. We came up with the same last name as Jane, but a first name of Mike. I gave Eileen the information I knew about Jane.

1. Jane X
2. Bensalem, PA
3. Lawyer
4. Divorced
5. Millionaire Child

Eileen worked on the phone and found out that Jane X had been married to Mike X, but she was dead. Jane had had a sister, Joan. Eileen figured out the woman I met was Joan X, and she was assuming her deceased sister's identity.

Eileen then contacted the press secretary for the wealthy European family Jane claimed to have been from. She said she was writing a small piece on the family and had a simple question about the ages of the siblings. Jane/Joan did not meet the age range of any of the children, and all of them worked for the family company. No one in the family was named either Jane or Joan.

I asked my client for Jane's cell number, promising not to call her. Eileen determined it was a prepaid cell phone. Imagine that: a wealthy aristocrat using a prepaid cell. I don't think so. The only calls on the bill were to my client.

Eileen then pretexted Mike X, the alleged husband, and acquired his cell phone number, as well as all the phone numbers associated with the house.

My client's only point of contact with Jane was the prepaid cell phone he provided me. When we called the house, one answering machine stated that you reached Mike X. The other answering machine stated Joan X, and it was the same voice as the woman I met, sans the British accent.

This was all getting very strange.

Eileen investigated further by contacting the local police. She found there were never any complaints of pipe bombs or animals tossed on anybody's property in the town. With all this evidence, I called my client and told him everything. To make a long story short, he still saw the dollar signs. I told him I wanted nothing to do with this woman.

I think he probably wishes he had listened to me. Turns out this woman had schizophrenia. There was no money. There were no pipe bombs. He had wasted his time.

The moral of the story: Not everyone who disappears is doing it for rational reasons.

 After you've disappeared, take everyone you meet with a grain of salt.

It's not just crazies you have to worry about in this off-the-grid underworld. If you leave the country or go online to reach out to other disappearing enthusiasts like yourself, chances are you're going to meet a lot of crooks, too, and a lot of undercover law enforcement. I have a little motto I like to repeat to all of my clients:

 Assume everyone you meet is cop, criminal, or crazy until proven otherwise.

I learned to screen people early in my career as a disappearing consultant. You should develop that skill, too.

Some guy from Vegas e-mailed me out of the blue and asked me if I could help him disappear. "OK, tell me your story," I said.

He told me that he sold merchandise on eBay, and law enforcement had contacted him to let him know the merchandise was stolen. The Vegas man stated that he had had no idea about the hot radios and TV's, and now he was concerned about his supplier coming after him.

I really did not push for detail. I was happy to have a new client, so I conversed back and forth with him a bit. For some reason, he kept refusing to explain why his supplier was coming after him. He kept saying things like "I don't know" or "You never know."

An alarm went off in my head.

I decided to do a little background on my new Vegas client. Thank whatever or whoever is master of this universe that I did. Mr. Vegas was, in fact, about to go on trial for several counts of receiving stolen merchandise. I dug further and discovered that the Vegas boob had been buying merchandise from some law enforcement body that set up a sting. Of course his "supplier" was coming after him—his supplier had been the police!

I confronted my felonious client and revealed my findings. "Does that mean you're not going to help me disappear?" he said.

Click. I hung up on him. That experience was a wake-up call telling me I need to know my client.

HOW TO WARD OFF CROOKS

When some criminal won't stop e-mailing me, I always write back, "Be aware that the feds are monitoring my e-mail." The F-word is like garlic to a vampire with those people. Works like a charm.

The world of the disappeared is full of people like Mr. Vegas. Another e-mail I got was from an anonymous writer with an address that was something like anarchist53992@hotmail.com. He asked if I could help him disappear. His story was that he had just come into a few hundred thousand dollars and did not want a new identity but wanted help getting the money offshore so no one could find the Benjamins or him.

My response was "get a tax attorney." He wrote back that he was not interested in going that route and emphasized his point by underlining "that route." Oookay. This told me he wanted something we in the business call a **"bag plan"**—that is, a plan for smuggling the money offshore.

Bag plan, n.: a scheme for moving money offshore illegally so that you don't pay any taxes on it. This is not something I teach people how to do.

I seriously doubt that Mr. Bag Plan was a real guy with a few hundred thousand Samoans. I would hope that someone with that kind of money lying around would be bright enough to plan a proper exit, not e-mail a stranger and risk his freedom. There's that old saying that two can keep a secret if one is dead. Murder's not a good idea, so:

Just keep your secrets to yourself.

As the years go by, you might get cocky about having managed to evade your pursuers. Resist the urge to brag—to friends and family from back home, to people you meet in the course of your new life, even to the bartender in the little bar in your Costa Rican village who can't possibly know what you're saying because he doesn't speak English . . . or does he?

You're never going to forget your past, so you should assume your pursuers won't, either. Have you ever seen or read *Les Misérables*? If not, I highly recommend that you do, paying close attention to the demented determination with which the police inspector Javert pursues Jean Valjean year after year after year. There's a reason that the Javert character is so compelling, and it's not just because of his soothing baritone. He reminds us that ghosts from the past have a way of coming back to haunt the present!

How do you stay vigilant as the years go by? Sign up for Google Alerts associated with your name and e-mail address, so you know if there are any changes about you in the public record. Change your location every couple of years, or as often as money and work commitments will allow. And finally: Have fun. Use your disappearance as an excuse to see the world, try new things, shake up your routine. When you leave your old life behind, you also abandon every excuse you ever had for not living the life you imagined.

More than anything else, the thing you should know about the world of the disappeared is this: It's a blank slate. What you write on it is entirely up to you.

PARTING WISDOM

Just remember: If two men in trench coats are at your door, it's the FBI. If it's just one man in a trench coat, it's the IRS. Either way, you probably shouldn't open the door.

ACKNOWLEDGMENTS

The authors want to acknowledge the people who helped make this book a reality. We thank Anna Sproul for her invaluable assistance in this project; Howard Yoon, our literary agent, who found such a great home for the book; Jody Hotchkiss; Reggae; and at the Globe Pequot Press, Steve Culpepper, who saw the value in our idea, and Kristen Mellitt, who helped us find our voice. Finally, Frank Ahearn is most grateful to his mother, Ann Ahearn, for being who she is.

INDEX